Pockets, Pullouts, and Hiding Places

Pockets, Pullouts, and Hiding Places

interactive elements for altered books, memory art, and collage

Jenn Mason

GLOUCESTER MASSACHUSETTS

QUARRY BOOKS

First published in the United States of America by:
Quarry Books, an imprint of
Rockport Publishers, Inc.
33 Commercial Street
Gloucester, Massachusetts 01930-5089
Telephone: (978) 282-9590
Fax: (978) 283-2742
www.rockpub.com

Library of Congress Cataloging-in-Publication Data

Mason, Jennifer.
    Pockets, pullouts, and hiding places : interactive elements for altered
books, memory art, and collage / Jennifer Mason.
            p.   cm.
    ISBN 1-59253-150-4 (pbk.)
    1. Paper work. 2. Pockets. 3. Scrapbooks. 4. Altered books. 5. Collage. I.
Title.
    TT870.M37328 2005
    745.54   dc22   2004022482
                                                                    CIP

ISBN 1-59253-150-4

10 9 8 7 6 5 4 3

Design: Dutton & Sherman
Cover Image: Allan Penn Photography

Printed in Singapore

The pages of this book are dedicated to the women who have made my life meaningful by letting me help them find their inner artist. Remember: she is able who thinks she is able.

contents

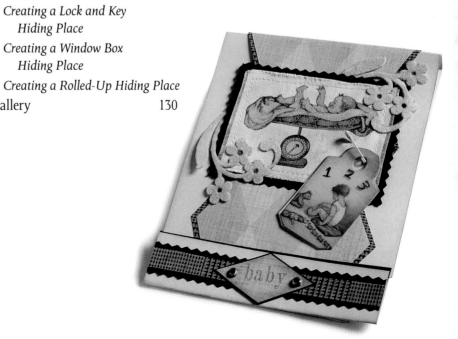

foreword

Are you a book artist, scrapbook designer, or aficionado of altered texts? If you are, prepare yourself for a whole new adventure! Jennifer Mason has compiled an exciting array of inspiring projects tailored just for you. *Pockets, Pullouts, and Hiding Places* is fresh, fun, innovative, and full of tips, ideas, and projects for paper artists at all skill levels.

The author's approach to book arts is sure to please even the most experienced artist or paper crafter. First, pockets: exciting, tantalizing, puzzling pockets! Who can resist opening one to disclose the contents? You might find almost anything inside—a love letter, a handwritten journal entry, a wedding announcement torn from the local newspaper, or an ancient map of a mysterious country. Discover how to add excitement to your next book project or scrapbook page by incorporating a variety of pockets into your design.

Next, pullouts: little treasures! A pullout could be a tiny, accordion-folded book encased in an altered text or a handmade artist book. It could be a scroll, a packet of old photographs, your great-grandmother's recipe cards, or any small handcrafted item. By adding treasures-within-treasures to your next handmade book, assemblage, or mixed-media art piece, you'll add layers of dimension and texture to your constructions while articulating your vision more clearly than ever. It's easy—with simple pullouts.

Finally, hiding places: perhaps the most tantalizing of all. Imagine deliberately concealing small pieces of artwork, handwritten text, vintage photos, and other treasures within your handcrafted book, scrapbook page, or three-dimensional art piece. How exciting for the viewer to participate in your art by discovering and unveiling the secret messages hidden inside! Potential hiding places might be holes, zippered enclosures, tiny envelopes tucked away in unexpected places, or any number of possibilities. Learn how to incorporate secret hideaways into your next project, adding mystery and intrigue to your art.

Many artists familiar to readers of *Somerset Studio* magazine have contributed their projects to this volume: Christine Adolph (Clear Pocket Collage, page 130), Linda Blinn (Ephemera Portfolio, page 132), Lynne Perrella (Envelope Journal, page 136), and Michelle Ward (Bee Journal, page 136), to name a few. Their creative suggestions will inspire you to try alternative ideas and apply fresh, innovative approaches to altered books, journals, scrapbook pages, and three-dimensional mixed-media artworks. Join Jennifer Mason and the contributing artists as they venture forth on a journey that never ends—one that begins with a pair of scissors, a gluepot, and your own creativity.

Sharilyn Miller

Sharilyn Miller serves as consulting editor to Somerset Studio *magazine and is the creator, founding editor, and Editor-in-Chief of* Belle Armoire *and* Art Doll Quarterly *magazines. She has published four books on jewelry making, rubber stamping, and paper arts, and teaches art workshops internationally.*

www.sharilynmiller.com

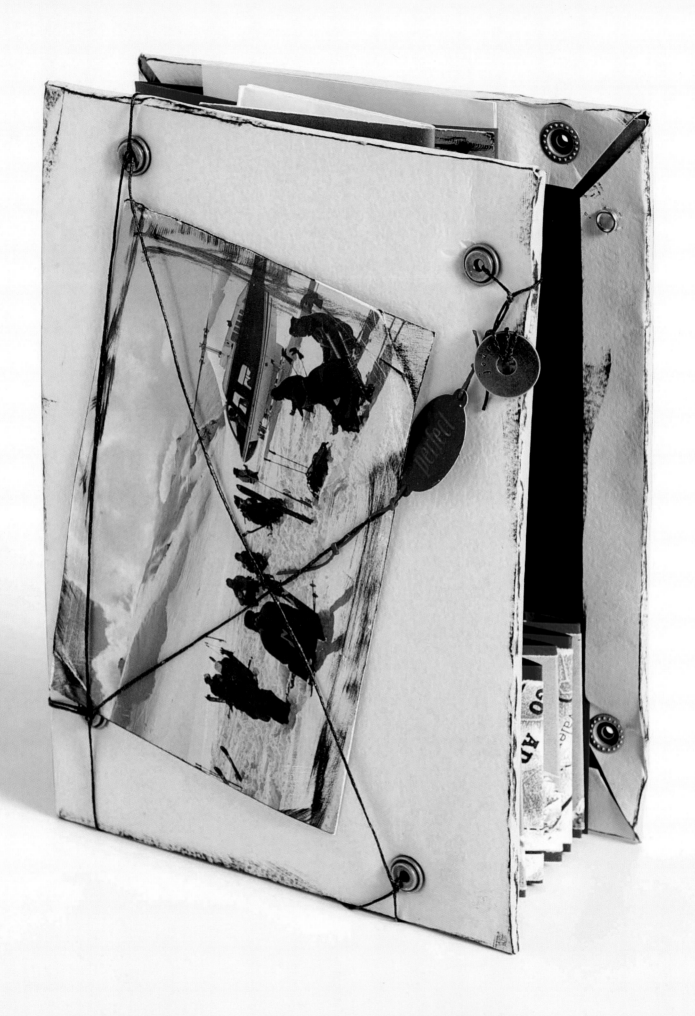

introduction

As a paper artist and a scrapbook designer who enjoys all things having to do with paper, I have watched the blending of several artistic disciplines over time. Scrapbook enthusiasts have branched out by using collage and altered art techniques to make memory art, and book and collage artists have been influenced by personal art journals and memory art. In this book I use the terms *artist* and *designer* freely because I feel that there is no single determining factor more important to becoming a designer or an artist than conceiving of and carrying out an idea. This book is for designers who enjoy working with scrapbooks, memory art, altered art, book arts, paper art, and collage, and for artists who enjoy all of the above.

In this book I've assembled a visual collection of what I call paper "tools" that can transform your designs and artwork from the two-dimensional and static to the three-dimensional and interactive. These tools can be both useful and visually appealing additions to your work. Pockets, pullouts, and hiding places can be used to harbor or conceal journaling, handwritten letters, a collection of quotes, additional imagery, important but less-than-perfect photos, and all types of ephemera and memorabilia including tickets, brochures, small souvenirs, and collections.

This book is divided into three main sections: Using the Written Word, Using Imagery, and Using Ephemera. Each of these sections is then divided into three different types of tools: Pockets, Pullouts, and Hiding Places.

These three types of tools are closely related, but I define them as follows:

- A pocket tool is a holding device, such as an open-ended envelope used to hold a love letter or a vintage report card.
- A pullout either pulls, opens, or flips with little or nothing holding it closed, such as a miniature book placed in a shadow box on a scrapbook page.
- Hiding places need to be uncovered, undone, or untied to be revealed, making them perfect for concealing secrets in your work.

There are twenty-seven basic tools included in this book. I present each one as a blank canvas, and then follow with specific projects that incorporate the tool. For further inspiration, at the end of each section is a gallery of work from contributing artists and designers who took the corresponding tool, molded it to their personal style, and added it to their own unique pieces.

In their simplicity, these interactive paper tools are timeless. They can be used in any kind of journal, scrapbook, or memory and paper art, regardless of its theme or style, offering the artist an exciting journey into the world of three dimensions.

I hope you are not only inspired to apply the tools in this book to your designs and art, but also to embrace them, mold them, and make them your own.

Longmont
Colorado
Sunflower
fields

chapter 1 tools and techniques

basic supplies

Every tool in this book, as well as the corresponding project ideas and gallery projects, contains a list of suggested materials. Listed here are supplies used throughout the book that are helpful to have on hand. Experienced paper artists know that there are usually at least two ways to do just about anything, so if you don't have a supply or tool that's listed on these pages, try to think of an alternative that might work just as well. You may even find a tool or supply that works better because there are always new products on the market that are worth trying.

paper

Throughout this book, many different types of paper are used: cardstock, vellum, decorative papers, acetate, shrink plastic, cork, tissue paper, and handmade paper. Remember to look beyond the obvious: try corrugated cardboard, color-copied ephemera, wood veneer, metal, or fabric as substitutes for paper.

tools of the trade

Cutting tools such as scissors, craft knives, and desktop paper trimmers for cutting multiple sheets are essential for the paper artist. For more interesting edges and cuts, try one of the many decorative-edged scissors available, rotary blades that cut perforations, or a metal tearing ruler. Don't forget that rotary blades and craft knives require a cutting mat beneath the paper or project.

Other tools of the trade, such as bone folders, rulers, sanding blocks or sand paper, hole punches, shape punches, crimpers, eyelet setting tools with mat, and a needle tool or bookbinder's awl, can help make the task at hand easier.

Specialized tools, such as a heat tool with interchangeable tips (especially useful for cutting foam core and making plastic pockets) and an embossing gun (for melting embossing powder, setting inks, and shrinking plastic) are also used in this book.

embellishments

There are untold numbers of embellishments you can use in your work, including brads, eyelets, staples, ribbons, fibers, clips, frames, alphabets, pins, and charms. When looking for embellishments, wander outside the paper arts store and into home improvement, sewing, and office supply stores: there is sure to be something just perfect for your next project.

adhesives

For putting it all together, you will need adhesives such as glue sticks, foam tape squares, spray adhesive, adhesive tape runners, adhesive sheets, double-stick tape, removable double-stick tape, industrial strength tape, and vellum adhesive. Most artists have favorite adhesives, but trying new ones may lead to discovering new favorites.

adding color

For coloring and customizing your work, inks (dye, pigment, and permanent), stamps (alphabets, numbers, dates, and images), stickers, embossing powder, pens and markers, paints (acrylic grounds, soft gel gloss, gesso, fluid acrylics, to name a few), and brushes, will come in handy. Experimentation with these supplies can give amazing outcomes. Try using paints intended for canvas on a book cover instead, press stamps into hot shrink plastic, or ink over an entire sheet of paper to change its color.

ephemera

Ephemera (tickets, shells, mail, feathers, or brochures) are always fun to collect and even more fun to use! Antique malls and flea markets are good places to find old letters, game pieces, and other fun ephemera. Consider making color copies of special keepsakes to use for multiple projects and to preserve for future use.

covering book boards

Many of the projects in this book start with covered book boards, which are used as book covers. This technique is relatively easy and gives a wonderfully finished feel to a project.

1. Start with a piece of mat board cut to the desired size. Mat fragments are usually marked down considerably and are often available at craft or hobby stores. Cut a piece of decorative paper bigger than the mat board so that the edges can fold over.
2. Glue the paper to the mat board using a bone folder to smooth the paper and the board together and to ensure good adhesion. Do not fold the edges over yet. Miter the four corners out of the paper, leaving a small amount of paper hanging over each edge.
3. Glue and wrap each paper tab over the mat board, using a bone folder to make good contact between the board and the paper.
4. Then run your bone folder along each edge to create nice crisp lines.

cutting shadow boxes

Some of the projects in the book are based on shadow boxes, and many of the pull-outs shown in this book can easily be added to one of these shadow boxes.

1. Measure the desired box shape on a piece of foam core. Place the foam core on a glass mat. Using a metal ruler and either a very sharp craft knife or a heat tool with a blade tip, cut out a hole. This will take a couple of passes with a regular craft knife.
2. Trace the hole in the foam core onto a cover sheet. Cut along the inside of the traced line for a slightly smaller hole so that the foam core edge will be hidden.
3. This example shows eyelets being used to attach ribbons (or fibers or elastics) to hold your shadow box contents in place.
4. This shadow box example is created by gluing torn sheets of layered vellum between the cover sheet and foam core to form a pocket. Try sandwiching holding devices and embellishments between the foam core and the cover sheet.

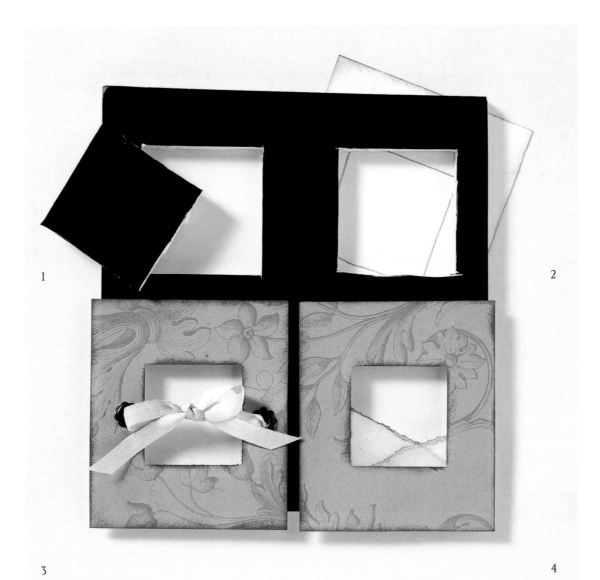

folding an accordion

The accordion is the base of many projects in this book. Scoring each page can be tiresome and folding paper back and forth, like making a fan, can result in an uneven accordion. Follow these directions for a relatively foolproof accordion every time.

For this example, the accordion will be folded into eight panels, so each panel will be 1/8 of your page size. If you don't need eight panels, it is still generally easier to evenly fold all eight sections and cut off the panels you don't need. If you need more than eight panels, two or more accordions can be attached by overlapping one panel with another one with a glue stick.

For each of these steps, use a bone folder to get a good crease.

1. Cut a strip of paper. Fold the strip of paper in half.
2. Open the strip and align each end with the middle crease.
3. Open and turn the strip over so that the three mountain fold peaks face up.
4. Bring both side folds to the center mountain fold, and crease the underneath layer.
5. Align both ends of the paper with the center mountain fold and crease.

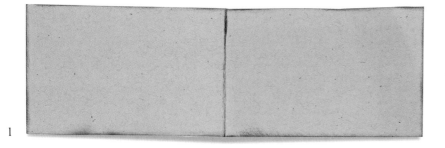

1

2

3

4

5

distressing photos and paper

Many of the projects in this book call for distressing photos or paper with ink, a sponge dauber, and a sanding block or sandpaper. It's easy to create a perfect customized look for a project by simply varying ink colors and the degree of distressing.

1. To distress a photo, start with a new photo and trim as needed.
2. Next, lightly ink the edges with a sponge dauber.
3. Crumple and sand the photograph as desired.

a. To distress paper, trim sheet of paper as needed.
b. Next, crumple then flatten the paper.
c. Rub an ink pad over the paper and the ink will transfer to the raised area.

To create an even more worn look, sand the edges and the surface of the paper to break up some of the fibers. This works especially well with dark paper that has a lighter core color.

chapter 2 using the written word

I have always felt there was value in including your own handwriting in your work. Imagine the thrill of finding a great-grandmother's note in an old Victorian scrapbook. When we are creating art to last, we have the opportunity to pass on memories to our family in a most intimate way— through our handwriting.

I also think that there is a great need, and, thankfully, a changing trend, to include more of the written word, and more heartfelt journaling, in one's work. Who, What, and When are always important, but it is the Why and How that a future audience may enjoy most.

Use the tools in these chapters to find ways to incorporate the intimacy of handwriting into your work. Invite future generations to interact with you through your art. Let them flip through your thoughts and stay a while.

pockets for written words

Ideas for elements to include in pockets:

- *Old report cards*
- *Love notes*
- *Small gift cards*
- *Recipes*
- *Correspondence*

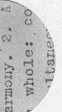

creating a
page pocket

The Page Pocket is an excellent way to incorporate a large amount of text into a project without detracting from the overall form. Slide in certificates of achievement behind a corresponding scrapbook page or slip some meaningful journaling in a Page Pocket for someone to read at her leisure. Try making the Page Pocket deeper using foam core or fun foam to make a pocket that can hold multiple secrets (see Diary of a Secret Princess Altered Book, pages 22–23).

materials

cardstock

adhesive

tools

circle punch

scissors

paper trimmer

instructions

To create a Page Pocket, you can either add a page pocket on top of a project surface, or use the actual paper from a journal or book page to craft it.

If you are using the project page itself, such as a page from an altered book, glue down three of the four sides of the first book page to the page behind it. Using a hole punch, add a thumbhole along the open side for removing the contents of the pocket.

If you are adding a separate page pocket to an existing project, cut a piece of sturdy paper or cardstock slightly larger than the finished pocket needs to be.

Punch a thumbhole on the side that will remain open.

Fold over a small tab on the remaining three sides and glue them down to the project page.

materials

old hardcover children's book
cardstock
foam core
decorative paper
tissue paper
handmade paper
glassine envelope
printed acetate
ribbon
paper flowers
flower eyelets
alphabet charms
glitter icicles
trim
soft gel gloss
fluid acrylics
inks
industrial strength tape
glue stick
photograph(s)

tools

sponge dauber
stamps
circle punch
craft knife
scissors
paper trimmer
bone folder

page pocket project idea:

diary of a secret princess altered book

Altered books can be made using a variety of surfaces, from a child's board book to a distressed copy of *War and Peace*. In this book, the guts have been removed to make room for a deep Page Pocket that is holding three different tabbed pullouts. Fun fibers and acrylic paints, gel mediums, and glitter make this an altered book fit for a princess!

instructions

Remove the inside pages from a book (save the pages for a future project). Mix fluid acrylics with soft gel gloss and paint the outside of the book cover. While the paint is still wet, add torn pieces of colored tissue paper and glitter icicles. Embellish the cover with charm letters and trim. Cut out a window in the front cover with a craft knife and glue torn decorative paper around the opening.

To create endpapers (these are the papers that are glued over the inside of a book cover to create a finished surface), distress decorative paper (see Distressing Photos and Paper, page 17). Cut the paper slightly smaller than the inside of the entire book cover; cut out the window area. Lay acetate over the window on the inside of the cover, then glue the distressed paper over it. Smooth with a bone folder to ensure good contact between the paper and the cover and score the folds on the inside of the spine. Glue a piece of acetate to the inside of the back cover for decoration.

To create the Page Pocket, cut three narrow strips of foam core for the three closed sides of your pocket. Glue them to the inside back cover. Decorate the paper for your Page Pocket with inks or other embellishments. Cut out the center of the paper to create a frame, punch thumbholes at the top, and glue over the foam core strips.

Crop photos to fit in the pocket; add collage elements and circle tabs if desired. Back the photos with cardstock to strengthen them and insert them into Page Pocket.

creating a
library pocket

The Library Pocket may bring back memories of your school days, and it is also a very utilitarian tool. Use it to tuck old love letters or bits of ephemera into your artwork. Add a door (see Aline Scrapbook Page, page 51) or a second pocket to add versatility. And of course, you can use this pocket to hold almost any kind of pullout.

materials
cardstock

adhesive

template (see page 138)

tools
bone folder

scissors

paper trimmer

instructions

Trace the template on cardstock and cut out. Score and fold the tabs; glue into place.

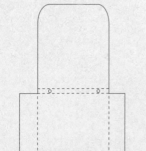

library pocket project idea:

lucy locket's pocket purse

If one Library Pocket is good then two is better! This fun little purse can also be a business card holder, and it is a great way to showcase personal style. Try making this project bigger to make extra special gift wrap, or make it smaller for a necklace pendant. This project is the perfect chance to use a treasured piece of beaded trim.

(continued on next page)

materials

cardstock
decorative paper
vellum
beaded trim
brads
flower nail head
eyelets
ribbon
permanent ink
double-stick tape
strong adhesive
template (see page 138)

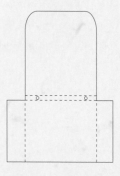

tools

sponge dauber
bone folder
craft knife
scissors
eyelet setting tools
paper trimmer

(continued from previous page)

instructions

Glue decorative paper to cardstock and smooth using a bone folder. Trace the template twice on the back of the paper, score fold lines, and cut out both pockets. Punch holes in the pocket bottoms and add eyelets. Add a vellum pocket with brads to the back of one pocket. Add embellishments aged with ink, then secure tabs with double-stick tape to create the first pocket.

For the second pocket, add a strip of decorative paper to the top front edge. Add a flower nail head to the center of the decorative strip. Secure pocket tabs with double stick tape and finish adhering decorative strip to the back of the pocket.

Thread ribbon through both Library Pockets. The top pocket faces forward and is upside-down. The bottom pocket faces backwards and is right side up. Secure the ribbon at the bottom with a bead and a knot on each side; cut off excess. Attach beaded trim using strong adhesive.

creating a
vellum pocket

Sometimes there is nothing more provocative than a subtle glimpse into the unknown. These handy Vellum Pockets can soften the look of a handwritten note, take the edge off a computer-printed message, or create an intriguing sleeve for a beautiful invitation.

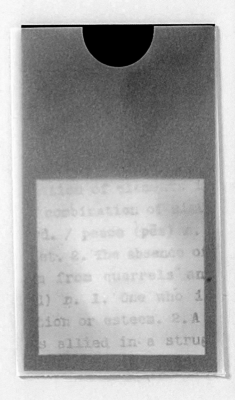

materials

vellum

vellum adhesive

tools

ruler

scoring tool

circle punch

decorative-edged scissors

scissors

instructions

Measure the width and the height of the item that will be held in the Vellum Pocket. Cut a piece of vellum that is twice the width plus $5/8$" (1.6 cm) and is the height of the item plus $1/2$" (1.3 cm). From the left edge, measure and score a line that is the width plus $1/8$" (0.3 cm). This will be the back panel. From the right and bottom edge, measure and score a fold line $1/2$" (1.3 cm) away from each edge to create tabs. Cut the bottom tab from the back panel portion. Diagonally cut the corners off the remaining tabs to make mitered corners. This helps create a clean, finished pocket without extra bulk.

To create a fingerhole, punch half a circle from the top front panel of the pocket. Fold the tabs to the back and secure to the pocket to the background surface with vellum adhesive. Pocket tops can be torn, trimmed with decorative-edged scissors, or accented with paper or ribbon trim.

To create a second pocket layer, cut a piece of vellum or other paper to the same width as the first pocket and the desired height plus $1/2$" (1.3 cm). Score the folds, cut the tabs, and punch finger hole, as described above. Fold both pockets together and secure both layers of tabs with vellum adhesive.

materials

vellum
cardstock
decorative paper
handmade paper
mat board
colored key tag
small tag
journal text
page pebbles
paper flower
elastic cord
metal word plates
nail heads
ink
colored pencils
pencils
adhesive
vellum adhesive
template (see page 138)
photograph(s)

tools

bone folder
scissors
paper trimmer

vellum pocket project idea:

cowgirl memory book

The Vellum Pocket is a versatile tool; it can be used as a sleeve, or even as a page. In this project, a pocket of beautiful printed vellum forms the page in a small memory book. Consider personalizing plain vellum pages with stamping and other surface treatments. This is a great project to give to far-off family members, especially to commemorate a special moment in time.

instructions

Using the template (page 138), make two identical Vellum Pockets. Cut two pieces of cardstock to the same size as the finished pockets. Cut two pieces of decorative paper (for endpapers) and two pieces of mat board (for covers), each $1/4$" (0.6 cm) taller and wider than the finished pockets. Cut handmade paper to the same height as the mat board and a width of 11" (27.9 cm).

Fold the handmade paper into eight accordion folds (see Folding an Accordion, page 16). Fold each of the sections of the accordion (except the first and last) in half again. Unfold the accordion and refold to create alternating mountain and valley folds.

Distress the outside of the mat boards with ink. Add small pictures and embellishments to the cardstock and vellum pages.

Adhere the first accordion section to the front mat board cover and the last to the outside back cover. Adhere the endpapers to the inside of the covers, then glue the first and inside panels to the inside front cover and the last panel to the inside back cover.

Alternate cardstock and vellum pages, and adhere them to the front-facing sides of the accordion panels. Adhere small pictures and embellishments to the backs of the cardstock pages. Insert journaling or text into the vellum pockets. Create a closure with a loop of elastic cord and embellishments, and then wrap it around the book to hold it closed.

pullouts for written words

Ideas for elements to include in pullouts:

- *Favorite quotes*
- *Love or chore coupon*
- *A child's handwriting from year to year*
- *Baby milestones*
- *Poems*
- *Collected autographs*

tag book pullout

materials

cardstock

tags (pre-made, punched, die cut, or traced from supplied template, page 139)

attachments (brads, eyelets, snaps, or staples)

tools

hole punch or craft knife

scissors

template (page 139)

Create tags and stack them to create mini booklets. This is a great way to showcase a stack of quotes, autographs, dates, or captions.

instructions

Tag pages can either be purchased or made using a punch, die cutter, or the template on page 139. Create front and back covers for the book using a contrasting or heavier paper stock. Add personalized text and any decoration to the tag pages, then secure them together with the front and back covers using brads, eyelets, snaps, or staples. As an alternative, try creating a tag book that swings open (see the Swing Pullout Tool, page 37).

materials

shrink plastic (inkjet printable for computer users)
cardstock
two-sided decorative paper
slide holder
message bottle
typewriter key frame
eyelets
metal spine
fibers
bath salts
ribbon charms
printed ribbon
children's illustration
stickers
dimensional glaze
ink, solvent based
decorative staples
embossing powder
chalks
cardboard letter stencil
adhesive
double stick removable tape
foam dots

tools

computer and printer, or alphabet stamps (for journaling)
assorted rubber stamps
hole punch
stapler
decorative punches (heart, circle, shoe)
eyelet setting tool
craft knife
cutting mat
decorative-edged scissors
scissors
paper trimmer

tag book pullout project idea:

tokens of friendship pullout mini book

The text kept in a pullout can be handwriting, journaling, autographs, favorite quotes, or as in this project, a book of gifts for a dear friend. These tokens are made from printable shrink plastic, but sanded shrink plastic and alphabet stamps can also be used to print the lettering. Remember that shrink plastic will reduce to a little less than 50 percent of its original size. Use removable double-stick tape to adhere the tokens so they can be easily removed from the pages.

instructions for computer journaling

Use page layout software program to design tokens. Use text manipulating software to create circular text. Print the tokens on the shrink plastic.

instructions for hand-stamped journaling

Use solvent-based inks to stamp the message directly onto the shrink plastic. Color the tokens with chalks.

Cut out the tokens from shrink plastic with small postage stamp or pinking shear decorative-edged scissors. Using a craft knife, cut a square out of each token's center. Stamp the tokens' backs, then shrink them, following the manufacturer's instructions.

general instructions

Cut identically sized pages and covers out of two-sided decorative paper. Decorate the front cover with stamps. Use stickers to create words on the right edge of each page. Use adhesive and foam squares to add other embellishments such as covered slide holders, punched shapes, stencils, stamped quotes, stapled printed ribbon, and collage materials to decorate the pages. Use removable double-stick tape to add the tokens to the pages.

Punch two holes through the covers and all of the pages. Insert eyelets in the holes of the front cover. Use a wired string or other strong fiber to attach the entire book to the metal spine, and tie it off in the back of the book.

Stamp and emboss the message bottle; fill with bath salts. Tie fibers and the bottle to the metal spine.

Create a title block using layered papers, stamps, and a computer if desired. Put a punched and decorated circle into a typewriter key frame and fill with dimensional glaze; let dry. Adhere the title block to the front cover of the book.

creating a
flap pullout

Turn just about any matted photo on a scrapbook page into a flap or add hidden pages in a handmade or altered book. Because it's so easy to construct, this is a great tool for those who have just begun to explore adding interactive elements to their artwork.

materials

cardstock

eyelets

tools

hole punch

eyelet setting tool

scissors

paper trimmer

instructions

Decide the size of the final closed flap, then double the length or the width; measure and cut from cardstock. Fold in half to create a flap and secure the back half to the project with adhesive or embellishments such as brads, eyelets, staples, hinges, or a combination of all four. Try adding a pull-tab (see above, lower right) or thumbhole to the flap to cue the reader. A variety of finished flaps are shown above.

flap pullout project idea:

sunflower fields altered book

For those who have always wanted to try altering a book but didn't know where to start (or have already tried altering a "grown-up" book), now may be the time to try altering a children's board book. They have sturdy pages that are fairly easy to cut; and with a glue stick, a craft knife, and some paper scraps, you can add flap pullouts and hidden elements in a flash.

instructions

Using a glue stick, craft knife, and bone folder, cover the outside of the book with decorative paper. Trim the paper along the edge of the board. Use a separate piece of paper to cover the spine and embellish with stickers. Sandwich ribbon ties between the cover and first page and the back cover and the last page, by gluing page to cover.

(continued on next page)

materials

decorative paper
ribbon
ribbon charms
charm plaques
bow
stickers
rub-ons
paper flowers
black pen
glue stick

tools

craft knife
scissors
bone folder

(continued from previous page)

Alter the pages and cover them with decorative paper. In this book, the first page is glued to the cover, the next page is cut in half, and the following page has one quarter cut off. There are three main pages with flaps and hiding places that are actually made using four pages: the first page has a flap cut in it (a rectangle cut on three sides and scored on the fourth side), followed by two pages with rectangular windows, cut slightly larger than the flap; these are glued together and then to a fourth page, where the back of the flap pullout is attached. (See photo on page 35.)

Add stickers, ribbons, and embellishments as desired throughout the book and in the sections under the flaps.

creating an
accordion pullout

For an easy but impressive addition to an art project, try the Accordion Pullout. Make it large or small, thin or wide; at any size this tool is a powerhouse. Wrap the tool closed with a gorgeous ribbon, or cinch it closed by slipping a decorated rubber band around the covers. Use decorated mat board, or sew a number of pieces of paper together to create a cover. For a simpler version, just leave the cover out. Because the Accordion Pullout is so versatile, it can fit into almost any project.

materials

cardstock

decorative paper

mat board

metal frames

glue stick

tools

bone folder

scissors

paper trimmer

ruler

instructions

Decide on the finished open size of your Accordion Pullout, then cut the paper to this size. Fold your accordion using a scoring tool and a ruler (see Folding an Accordion, page 16).

To make covers, cut two pieces of mat board approximately ¼" (0.6 cm) wider and taller than the folded accordion pages. Cut two pieces of decorative paper at least 1" (2.5 cm) wider and taller than the mat boards. Adhere the paper to the front of the boards and fold over the excess to the back (see Covering Book Boards, page 14).

Glue the accordion, centered, to the front and back covers. Cut and glue decorative endpaper to the insides of the covers to conceal the construction.

materials

cardstock
handmade or decorative paper
watercolor paper
foam core
clear frame stickers
paper flowers
brads
ribbon
ink
water color paint and brush
removable double-stick tape
industrial strength double-stick tape

tools

metal ruler
stamps
alphabet stamps
craft knife
scissors
paper trimmer
sewing machine

accordion pullout project idea:

melanie's smile memory art book

Try combining favorite quotes with special photos in a lovely accordion book. This kind of book presents a number of decorating options, making it easy to expand and explore creativity while making a wonderful keepsake. Use ribbon to call attention to an accent in a photo, or use special handmade paper to convey a specific place and time. Embellish simply or lavishly—the choice is yours.

instructions

Choose three coordinating papers for the covers (two sheets of card-stock and one handmade or decorative paper) and cut two 5" × 7" (12.7 × 17.8 cm) pieces from each. Crumple and flatten the cardstock for the inside covers.

Measure and mark a 6" × 20" (15.2 × 50.8 cm) strip of water-color paper. Using a metal ruler pressed along the marked line, lift the paper against the ruler and tear to create soft edges all around.

Fold the accordion paper in half and score every 4" (10.2 cm) from the middle. There will be 2" (5.1 cm) remaining on either side.

Paint large swatches of color on the paper using watercolors.

Cut a 3 1/4" × 5" (8.3 × 12.7 cm) piece of foam core, then cut a 2 1/4" × 3 3/4" (5.8 × 9.6 cm) hole from the center; save it for the front cover.

Stamp a "made with LOVE" tag on a small scrap of paper.

for the front cover

Layer from bottom to top: one of the pieces of cardstock, a piece of the handmade paper, the cut-out foam core, the front flap of the accordion paper, the crumpled cardstock, and the stamped tag. With a sewing machine, zigzag stitch around the perimeter, approximately 1/4" (0.6 cm) from outside edge.

for the book

To create the foam core shadow box, cut a small hole in the middle of the inside back cover. Peel back the cardstock to reveal the opening in the foam core. Place the clear frame sticker over a photo, cut out the center portion of the photo, and glue into the shadow box frame. Cut out along the outside of the sticker and glue the frame to the outside of the shadow box, letting some of the torn edge show inside the frame.

Sew the remaining photos to the pages with a sewing machine. Stamp and embellish the rest of the accordion pullout.

Create a buckle for the front of the cover by adhering a circle frame sticker to a scrap of the handmade paper. Cut out two strips from a frame sticker to make the center part of the buckle. Trim down and adhere one of the strips to fit in the center of the buckle. Cut out the excess paper from the buckle openings. Reinforce the center of the buckle by placing the second strip over the back. Adhere the buckle to the ribbon on the left side; fold over and secure with industrial strength double-stick tape. Close the book by looping the right side ribbon through the buckle.

hiding places for written words

Ideas for elements to include in hiding places:

- *Love letters*
- *A teacher's note*
- *A reduced copy of a certificate*
- *A list of gifts received*
- *Journaled dreams*
- *Secret wishes*

creating a
sealed envelope hiding place

materials
cardstock

envelopes

wax seals (real or faux)

stickers

photo corners

pen

Art can be extremely personal. Use this tool to keep meaningful information private, so that not everyone can see or read it at a glance. Or use it to conceal a letter to future generations, a prize to be discovered at a later time. Whatever your intention, using a Sealed Envelope Hiding Place to store valuable secrets is as easy as licking the envelope. Just start with a ready-made envelope and embellish as desired.

instructions

As shown in the examples above:

Add a little humor by taping the envelope shut with a label made with a labelmaker to signal that you don't want anyone peeking (left). For a sophisticated approach, add the envelope to the project with the addressed side showing (center). For an elegant touch, use old-fashioned sealing wax (right). Use photo corners or beautiful ribbons to attach the envelopes to a surface.

materials

photographs
cardstock
decorative paper
ribbon
sticker seals
metal embellishments
conchos
rub-on letters
staples
ceramic tag
metal plaque
ink
printed twill tape
adhesive
plastic envelope template system
  (or unfolded envelope)
die-cut alphabet

tools

stapler
sanding block or sand paper
scissors
paper trimmer
sewing machine

sealed envelope hiding place project idea:

hunter cooks scrapbook page

Sometimes, the true story behind a scrapbook page is not the event in the pictures but something deeper. Certain pictures might speak of personality, personal drive, and will power. Tuck these messages into scrapbook pages in little sealed envelopes. Not only are they secure ways of sharing thoughts, they can also be delightful embellishments!

instructions

Adhere two photos slightly askew to two pieces of decorative paper cut slightly larger than the photo. Fold the edges of the paper over to create a mat, then zigzag stitch to secure; ink the edges to finish. Use three different papers to make envelopes using an envelope template; cut three top flaps to size from separate, but coordinating, paper. Place messages in the envelopes and seal with stickers. Sand the edges of two photographs and create a distressed mat for one of them (see Distressing Photos and Paper, page 17).

Create the background page using strips of decorative paper and cardstock. Attach photos and envelopes with embellishments. Die cut a portion of the title and cut small circles of decorative paper to fit in the conchos. Attach this to the page, then add the rest of the title using rub-on letters.

creating a
matchbook hiding place

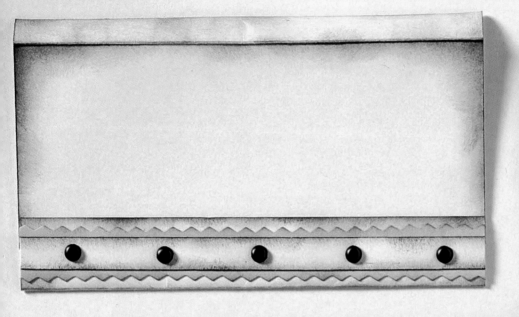

materials	tools
cardstock	stapler
brads	hole punch
jute	square punches
ink stamps	pinking scissors
	scissors
	paper trimmer

Matchbooks have been around for a long time. The tiny matchbooks that are often personalized for wedding favors or for restaurants can now be enlarged and embellished to create enclosures and innovative packaging for art. No template is needed for this power-packed little tool. All it takes is a simple strip of cardstock and a couple of well-placed scored lines to create the proper folds.

instructions

Cut the cardstock to desired width. To determine length, double the finished height of the matchbook and add approximately 1/4" to 1/2" (0.6 to 1.3 cm) for the top spine and 1/2" to 1" (1.3 to 2.5 cm) for the bottom flap. These are suggested measurements; use whatever works for the particular project.

After cutting the cardstock to the desired length, score the fold lines. The first score line is the bottom flap measurement; the next is the finished height; and the last is the spine.

Try making a practice matchbook with a scrap piece of paper first to determine the look and size. For variations, try leaving off the top spine or adding an accordion fold or two in the top instead.

Insert contents and secure the matchbook with fiber, a staple or two, or any number of brads; or, leave the bottom flap unsecured and wrap it with ribbon or a decorative rubber band so that the contents can be easily removed. If needed, shorten the front flap so that it tucks neatly into the bottom flap.

matchbook hiding place project idea:

babies and stress relief bubbles gift cards

Small gifts enclosed in a matchbook are wonderful little acts of kindness that evidence a love for paper arts. The Baby's 1sts book holds a list of important baby milestones. The Floral Bubble Wrap Matchbook is a delightful stress-relieving gift filled with removable sheets of bubble wrap and a prescription to pop one sheet every 4–6 hours. Think of some lovely note or small token to slip into one of these mini works of art.

instructions

For both books: Cut matchbook cover and decorative paper layers. Glue all of the main layers together, then score and fold the matchbook.

for baby's 1sts

Create the enclosure (below, left) by layering cardstock and decorative papers. Stamp and letter the embellishments; adhere them using adhesive and foam squares. Add brads, then secure the enclosure to the matchbook using strips of decorative paper, stamped embellishments, and brads.

For the front cover of the matchbook (below, right), print vintage clip art on inkjet-compatible fabric paper. Cut it out and fray the edge. Trim a piece of black cardstock with pinking shears and sew the fabric to it. Adhere to the matchbook. Cut out flowers from flocked vellum and glue to the cover. Add an acetate tag and an ink-sponged tag to the cover with a safety pin. Sponge the edge of the matchbook to add a little color.

(continued on next page)

materials

cardstock
decorative paper
inkjet-compatible fabric paper
vintage clip art
flocked vellum
acetate tag
ink-sponged tag
ribbon
charm
concho
square, decorative brads
safety pins
ink
adhesive
foam tape

tools

sponge dauber
sanding block or sand paper
square punch
pinking scissors
scissors
paper trimmer
sewing machine
computer and printer

(continued from previous page)

for the floral bubble wrap matchbook

Print vintage clip art on adhesive-backed paper. Age the clip art and the matchbook as desired with ink and a sponge dauber.

Adhere the clip art to the cover of the matchbook and to a piece of cardstock cut to fit the top flap. Punch out three squares from the cover and place the cardstock inside the match-box so that the clip art shows through the holes. Pull off the back legs of the three square,

decorative brads and adhere to the matchbook so they show through the cut out holes.

Distress a square concho embellishment with sandpaper. Attach it to the bottom flap making sure to catch the ribbon in the square. Close the flap and tie the ribbon securely around the bottom flap. Tie on the charm.

Slip two sheets of bubble wrap and the Stress Relief Prescription into the matchbook.

When you are stressed
and full of troubles
just grab a sheet and
pop some bubbles!
Watch problems go
with a loud 'pop! pop!'
soon your spirits will
be back on top.
This is therapeutic
and after a while
you'll find yourself
begin to smile!

Directions: Pop one sheet of stress relieving capsules every 4 - 6 hours or as needed.
Warning: May become addictive. In case of overdose please seek professional counseling.

creating a
reinforcement hiding place

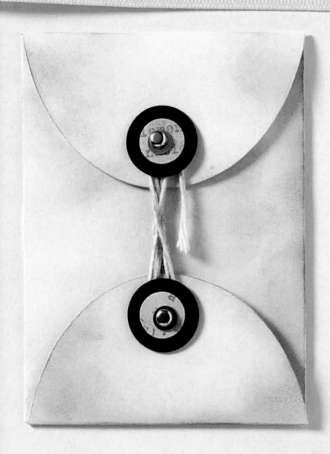

materials

cardstock

brads

tie (twine, raffia, yarn, or other fiber)

template (see page 139)

tools

circle punch

craft knife

scissors

paper trimmer

instructions

Punch out reinforcements using circle punches in varying sizes. Use the tip of a craft knife to make small holes in the center of the reinforcements, and through the paper or flap wherever they will be placed.

Cut the ties to a length approximately four times the distance between reinforcement placements. Make a small loop on one end of the tie and secure with an overhand knot. Trim the tail of the short thread. Slip one brad through the reinforcement, then through the small loop, then fasten it through the paper. Secure the other brad directly through the reinforcement and through the paper. Wrap the tie in a figure eight to close the hiding place.

This handy technique of using reinforcements to secure a secret is reminiscent of old confidential business envelopes. Use this tool to hide secret words tucked into a page or a handmade envelope (see Template, page 139).

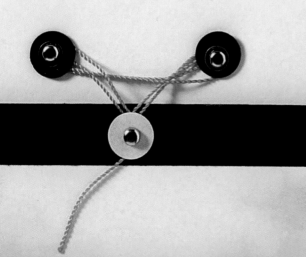

materials

cardstock
decorative paper
children's illustration
library due date slip
old playing card
label holder
photo turns
old map
canvas
stickers
eyelet snaps
brads
nails
jute
translucent embossing paste
matte gel medium
acrylic paints
acrylic extender
template (see page 140)

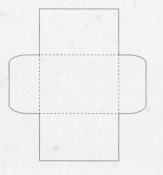

tools

mini label maker
graining tool
brass templates
hammer
craft knife
scissors
paper trimmer
paint brush

reinforcement hiding place project idea:

us 2 fishin' together

Because almost anything fits in these pockets, it's possible to combine text and ephemera by using the Reinforcement Hiding Place and a game card for a portion of the title. For those who enjoy working with three-dimensional embellishments but haven't worked on canvas yet, this is a great project to start with. If the canvas is going to be framed, work on any standard stretched canvas, but remember to leave a small margin free from embellishment to allow for the frame. It may help to trace lightly where the frame will cover the canvas before decorating it. If using an unframed, stretched canvas, choose one that is stapled in the back for a museum-quality look.

instructions

Mix the paint with the paint extender to create a transparent wash. Paint the canvas and leave color variations and brush marks showing. Paint a thin, transparent patch of a complimentary color, then run the graining tool through it to simulate wood texture.

Create a Reinforcement Hiding Place using the envelope template (see page 140) and an old map. Leave one long side of the Reinforcement Hiding Place open and tuck the other long side behind the two short flaps, which will be tied together. Distress and age the hiding place as desired and add the playing card, stickers, and label. Attach the hiding place to the canvas using photo turns and small nails.

Use embossing paste, the wood graining tool, and a brass stencil to create a textured image.

Distress the photos and illustration with paint, then adhere to the canvas with matte gel medium.

Attach remaining embellishments as desired.

materials

cardstock
decorative paper
tissue paper
papier-mâché box
printed transparencies
antique postcard
lace tags
mat board
ribbons
brads
metal frame
key
stamps
postcard tile
matchboxes
paper roses
stickers
cocoa ink
cream acrylic paint
adhesive

tools

Vellum Pocket (see page 27)
sponge
scissors
paper trimmer
paint brush

instructions

Base coat the box with cream acrylic paint. Adhere crumpled tissue paper to box and sponge with cocoa ink. Line the inside of the box with papers and transparencies. Embellish the box with lace, brads, papers, tags, ribbons, and trims. Layer postcard, prepared tag, vellum pocket, metal frame, and stamped scripts and adhere to cover. Fill the box with a small treasure box accordion book (developed by Tana Mitchell) and special keepsakes.

To make the treasure box accordion book, cut and cover three mat board panels slightly larger than the length and width of two matchboxes laid end to end. Cut a piece of cardstock four times the width of the matchbooks and the same length as the two matchbooks laid end to end. Fold this cardstock into four segments. Starting with one board on the bottom, layer a ribbon (for tying the book closed), two matchboxes laid end to end with beaded and wired knobs facing out, the second board, the accordion cardstock, and the final covered board. Embellish with Vellum Pocket and other elements as desired.

words give our hearts wings papier-mâché book box

Michelle Bodensteiner

The addition of Vellum Pockets (see page 27) softens the work and complements the historical tone of this book box and ephemera.

altered book with paper bag pocket (bottom right)

Beth Cote

This Page Pocket (see page 21) seems to grow right out of the book with the use of burned and torn edges.

aline scrapbook page (standing)

Jeannine Stein

On this lovely page, the Library Pocket (see page 24) does triple duty by holding a tag, concealing a photo, and featuring a decorative pop-up.

instructions

Layer patterned paper onto cardstock. Create a photo frame with painted strips of copper mesh attached with brads. Sand and paint metal letters and attach with brads.

Create pockets from template and decorate using stamps, circle punch, and a photo. To create the pop-ups for inside the pocket doors, cut a strip of paper $1/2$" $\times$ 3 $3/4$" (1.3 cm $\times$ 9.6 cm), score it every $3/4$" (1.9 cm), and fold the strip into a square; adhere the overlapping sections. Attach the square to the inside of the flap with an attached text or image. Make sure the pop-up doesn't extend beyond the pocket when closed.

materials

altered book
kraft paper bag
clip art from *The Ephemera Book* or *CD* by Beth Cote
decorative paper and vellum
craft cork
slide mounts
rickrack
old button and vintage earring parts
vintage file folder
tea-stained tags
adhesive stamps
chalk ink
glue

tools

fine sandpaper
hole punch
scissors
paper trimmer

instructions

Rip two pages in the altered book. Burn the edges of the paper carefully over a kitchen sink full of water.

Size the paper bag to fit the book and glue the paper bag between the pages. Rub chalk ink gently over the paper; rip it to fit the front of the pocket and glue to page. Rip the vellum slightly larger and glue to page. Cut file folder to fit inside of the pocket; embellish with ledger paper, leftover paper, and journaling.

Glue on the image from the clip art book or CD, rickrack, and three-dimensional objects. Stamp on tags. Add a bit of vellum inside a slide mount and sand with fine sandpaper. Punch a hole and hang from file folder.

materials

cardstock
decorative paper
metal letters
copper mesh
brads
paper flowers photo turns
tassels
acrylic paint
adhesive
template (see page 141)

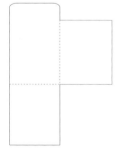

tools

foam stamps
rubber stamps
circle punch
scissors
paper trimmer

materials

cardstock
decorative papers
five tags
photographs
custom-folded cardstock, tile shape
rub-ons
brads
wire charm
photo corners
stickers
ink
adhesive
template (see page 140)

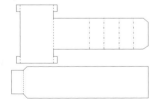

tools

label maker
pinking shears
paper crimper
rubber stamps
scissors
paper trimmer

4 days of drew scrapbook page

Karen Burniston

The Tag Book Pullout (see page 31) on this page has been ingeniously turned into an interactive journal of words and images.

instructions

Enlarge the tag book templates 200 percent and copy them onto stock. Cut out, and score on the dotted lines. Lay section A of template 2 under section A of template 1, with As facing the same direction, and glue. Decorate five tags with papers, photos, stamps, and rub-ons; spell a name by placing a letter on each tag end if desired. Attach the tags, in order, to the cardstock template by lining up a tag at each score line. Fold the long flap to the back and add hidden journaling.

Layer decorative paper onto cardstock to create the background; ink around the edges.

Attach the tag book to the page by folding in the B tabs and cutting slits in the layout; the slits should accommodate the rectangular area with the B tabs still folded in. On the back of the layout, unfold the tabs and adhere. Train the tag book by pulling the tags and pressing each one open to reinforce the folds. Add a "pull" tag to the back side of the journaling on template 2.

Add stamps, rub-ons, ink, and labels using a mask for the decorated rectangles. Add a photo, photo corners, and border stickers. Cut patterned paper with pinking shears; run through a paper crimper to create rickrack. Use rickrack to hold the heart charm; secure with brads and adhesive.

wedding day 1924

Dana DiCicco

Two leatherlike paper Flap Pullouts (see page 34) are pulled back to reveal two collaged portrait Flap Pullouts that conceal a map and journaling.

materials

cardstock
decorative paper
vellum
acetate
leatherlike paper
brass hinges
eyelets
ink
double-sided photo/document tape
craft adhesive

tools

stamps
scissors
paper trimmer

instructions

Make two color copies of each portrait and cut away the background from one of these pairs. Lay down a piece of patterned card stock right side up. Next, glue the two untrimmed portraits on the center of the layout, side by side. Cover this with the printed acetate, placing adhesive over the people in the pictures. (It will be covered by the next layer). Adhere the two cut-out portraits over the original two copies on the layout. To create the flaps, cut through all the layers, along the top, bottom, and center of the photos. Bend the flaps open and reinforce with hinges and eyelets. The doors open to reveal a stamped map inside. All layers are secured to a piece of cardstock. Here, the leatherlike flaps are cut to look like portrait holders; they are overlapped, hand sewn, and secured with small strips that are pulled through small slits in the overlapping section.

materials

quote book
book board
cardstock, assorted colors
decorative paper, assorted colors
color transparencies
organza ribbon
adhesive
small plastic bag

tools

bone folder
craft knife
paper trimmer

triangular accordion book

Holly Sar Dye

This triangular Accordion Pullout (see page 37) filled with quotes adds a twist to the standard folded accordion.

instructions

To make book covers, cut a 4 ½" (11.4 cm) square of book board in half diagonally to create two triangles. Cover the boards with paper and decorate with color transparencies. Glue two pieces of organza ribbon to the insides of the front and back covers.

Select various colors of decorative paper and cardstock. Cut five sheets of decorative paper to 4" × 8" (10.2 × 20.3 cm) for the accordion. Score each down the middle to make a valley fold with 4" × 4" (10.2 × 10.2 cm) panels. Cut four sheets of cardstock to 4" × 8 ¼" (10.2 cm × 21 cm); score and valley fold each ¼" (0.6 cm) in from the right side. Cut a 4" × 8" (10.2 × 20.4 cm) piece of cardstock. Fold all five pieces of cardstock down the middle so each has two 4" × 4" (10.2 × 10.2 cm) panels. Glue the five decorative sheets to the five pieces of cardstock on the valley fold side, leaving the tabs uncovered.

To make the accordion, fold under the bottom left corner of each left-hand panel. Be sure to line up the corners and score well with the bone folder. Fold under the bottom right corner of each right-hand panel (ignore the ¼" [0.6 cm] tab). Cover one of the tabs with adhesive and place a second panel on top of the tab (do not overlap the seam). Continue assembling the remaining panels in this fashion, attaching the panel with a tab last.

Align and glue the front cover to the first accordion panel. Align and glue back cover to last panel. Place folded book in a small plastic bag. Weigh down with one or two heavy books until dry. To finish, add quotations and tie ribbons.

what is life? collage

Cheryl Darrow

The use of copper mesh and buttons in this Reinforcement Hiding Place (see page 47) creates an artistic and textural collage.

instructions

Tear scrap papers and glue to cardstock or mat board. Dry brush acrylic paint followed by walnut ink on the paper. Dry brush off-white acrylic paint over the small frames and let dry.

Cut the copper mesh into an envelope shape, and cut strips for the edges of the layout. Dry brush the copper mesh with acrylic paint and let dry. Stamp copper mesh with acrylic paint to create large, repeating patterns. Fold the copper strips in half and attach to the edges of the layout using brads. Use the Japanese hole punch to make the holes for the brads.

Wrap the wire around the dowel to create a spiral. Remove the dowel and hammer the wire into a flattened spiral.

Insert lettered cardstock into the sections of the spiral and glue down (see the word "Experience").

Stamp a saying onto a piece of paper. Add ink to the background and fold into thirds; place inside the mesh envelope.

Finish envelope with buttons or other decorative elements. Glue the saying inside frames and assemble ribbon, frames, and envelopes; attach to the layout.

materials

cardstock
small frames
decorative paper
ribbon
copper mesh
brads
wire
acrylic paint
walnut ink
decoupage glue
adhesive
tape

tools

rubber stamp
paint brush
glue brush
Japanese hole punch
dowel
hammer
scissors

materials

cardstock
photograph
ribbon
book plate
bottle cap
rub-ons
epoxy numbers
safety pins
mini brads
woven label
vintage ledger paper
waxed linen thread
jewelry tags
ink
blue paint
adhesive

tools

stamps
scissors
paper trimmer

instructions

Layer a darker shade cardstock over the background cardstock. Layer a torn piece of ledger paper over the darker cardstock. Stamp a diamond pattern onto the background in black ink. Add computer-generated letters to the diamonds.

Add a photo and stapled woven label. Pierce the photo, and the right side of the background, then tie with waxed linen thread. Add three ribbons with adhesive and knot. Add rub-on embellished jewelry tags with safety pins. Stamp the swirl in black ink and color with blue paint.

Make a matchbook (see Matchbook Hiding Place, page 44). Add the bookplate and bottle cap (customized with rub-ons) to the cover using mini-brads. Add a message inside of the matchbook using rub-ons and embellishments.

"C"—christian james scrapbook page

Jenni Bowlin

The Matchbook Hiding Place (see page 44) on this scrapbook page adds an interactive complexity that engages the viewer.

we grow collage

Allison Strine

In this collage, which incorporates snippets of favorite outgrown childhood clothes, the Sealed Envelope Hiding Place (see page 41) becomes the "roots" of the jeweled flower.

instructions

Trim a piece of artist's canvas to size. Apply paints and pigment inks; heat set the pigment inks.

Create title by stamping white sailcloth fabric. Sew a photo mat using felt and denim. Use contrasting thread for visual interest, if desired. Sew denim fabric and trim around the edges. Add transparencies, burlap, lace, and flowers. Using an existing envelope as a template, create an envelope from sailcloth. Paint envelope, tuck a treasured note inside, and attach it to the flower stem.

materials

ribbon
flowers
transparencies
artist's canvas
sailcloth
felt
jeans
burlap
lace
earring
buttons
adhesive
paint
pigment inks

tools

scissors
paper trimmer
sewing machine (optional)
heat setting tool

chapter 3 using imagery

If a picture is worth a thousand words, then how many words can fit on a page? Five thousand? Twelve thousand? There is no real answer; but this chapter explores techniques for fitting more pictures on scrapbook pages, hiding pictures in memory art, and incorporating pictures into paper art. As in the other chapters, many of these projects are adaptable to something other than photographs. Try mixing and matching pockets with pullouts. Feel free to experiment with photographs using these elements as a starting point.

pockets for images

Ideas for elements to include in pockets:

- *Group photos*
- *Before and after photos*
- *Extra scenic photos*
- *Transparent Collaged Photos*
- *Copies of favorite artwork*
- *Copies of a child's handiwork*
- *Illustrations*
- *Cartoons*

creating a
lace-up pocket

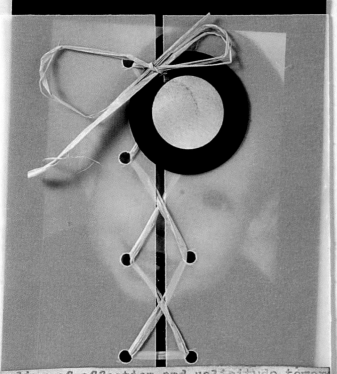

Make a softer, more feminine pocket with a little lacing. Using raffia, twine, jute, or shoelaces can change the look of a pocket. Because these pockets use a visual construction instead of hidden adhesive, the pockets can literally "tie" into a project!

materials

cardstock

adhesive

laces (raffia, twine, jute, or other fibers)

tools

bone folder

hole punch

scissors

paper trimmer

instructions

Measure the items planned for the pocket to determine the size. To overlap the pocket where the lacing appears, cut the pocket twice as wide as the contents plus 5/8" (1.6 cm). If you want space between the lacing for the contents to show through, as in the example above, cut the pocket twice as wide as the contents only. Cut the height of the pocket the same height as the contents or smaller, depending on the look you want. Fold pocket along scored lines.

Punch holes for lacing, remembering to either lace the bottom front to the bottom back, or add a trim or adhesive to secure the bottom. Select lace and sew up your pocket.

materials

cardstock
patterned paper, 2 sheets
ribbon
letter stickers
thin fiber
paper flower
printed journal boxes
small buttons
adhesive
templates (see pages 141–142)

tools

needle
stamp
hole punch
decorative-edged scissors
scissors
paper cutter

lace-up pocket project idea:

corseted pocket announcement

With a little ingenuity, a Laced-Up Pocket is turned into a baby announcement in a card that is "all girl." Choose bright flowery paper and write "Thanks for your support!" inside: the perfect sentiment when a gift is too much and a simple "thank you" is too little. Remember that lovely materials make lovely cards, so have fun combining beautiful ribbons and beautiful patterns.

instructions

Trace the card enclosure, template 2 (page 142) onto cardstock and cut it out. Trace the inside corset card, template 1 (page 141) on one sheet of patterned paper and the corset skirt, template 3 (page 142) onto the other sheet and cut them out. Use decorative-edged scissors along the top and bottom of the inside corset card.

Trace just the bottom half of the inside corset card template onto patterned paper. Cut out and glue onto the outside of the bottom of the corset card; be sure to leave a small amount of the decorative edge showing, and trim excess. Secure the inside of the corset card with buttons and thin fiber using a needle to pierce the paper. Decorate the journal boxes with stickers, text, and photos; slip into the inside corset card.

Score the corset skirt along the fold lines. Run a strip of adhesive along the top, then accordion fold the skirt along the scored lines, securing it to the adhesive. Glue to the bottom of the pocket.

Punch matching holes along the inside edges of the corset card with a hole punch. Use a large stamp to decorate the front of the card. Starting at the bottom holes, lace up the card and tie a bow at the top. Secure a small flower to the bow. Slip the inside corset card into the pocket.

it's a
girl

creating a
catch-all pocket

To add a bunch of removable items or to display a collection of items, use the Catch-All Pocket. Sew around the edge, or use other items such as staples, brads, or fibers to safely secure the pocket to a project.

The pocket doesn't have to be placed on the bottom of a project; try adding a corner or side pocket as well. For a more transparent look, try vellum or acetate.

materials

cardstock or vellum

waxed string

brads, staples, or fibers

tools

scissors

needle

sewing machine

instructions

Cut out pocket to the needed size. Add adhesive, embellishment, or fiber to the pocket edge. Hold securely in desired location. Sew or otherwise secure in place. To make hand sewing easier, try poking evenly spaced holes around the pocket with a piercing tool, such as a needle, before stitching.

catch-all project idea:

curls and cocoa petals

Use vellum instead of cardstock to create a see-through pocket like the one seen here. Crisp, clean lines; repetition of form; and bright colors are all playing a part in this cheery composition. The conchos secure the pocket to the page and also help reinforce the contemporary feel of this layout. Experiment with ways of attaching the pocket. Try choosing one to fit the style of a particular project or use a strong adhesive to attach the pocket without extra embellishment.

instructions

Cut the background paper, photo mats, extra embellishments, vellum, and titles; round the corners. Crop the photos; round the corners.

Adhere background to page. Adhere vellum to the page with conchos. (To adhere the vellum to the page, place a piece of craft foam under the page and push the prongs of the conchos through the paper and into the foam.)

(continued on next page)

materials

cardstock
decorative paper
vellum
alphabet stickers
conchos
waxed string
ball chain and connector
letter clips
markers
foam tape squares
matted photos

tools

bone folder or Popsicle stick
corner rounder
craft knife
cutting mat
scissors
paper trimmer

(continued from previous page)

To create the open conchos, turn the page over and bend over the prongs with a popsicle stick or bone folder. Push the prongs out (instead of in); cut out the centers carefully with a craft knife using the cutting mat.

Slip large matted pictures into the pocket. Add the title and title strips to the page. Add the remaining photos. Attach the tags to the last photo mat using open conchos, a paper strip, waxed string, and ball chain. Journal on the tags with markers and alphabet stickers. Adhere the photo mat and tags to the page with foam tape squares for dimension. Add the letter clips to the pocket.

This pocket is a fun tool for anyone's arsenal and inspirational creative bank. By itself it can hold love letters, photos, or a collection of homemade cards or recipes—or use it in a project to hold lots of creative goodies. Make it with three envelopes or twenty!

materials

envelopes

(or envelope template, page 140)

glue

tools

scissors

paper trimmer

instructions

Assemble envelopes and cut off the top flaps. If desired, use an envelope template (see page 140) or an unassembled envelope to make custom pockets.

Line up the envelopes. Apply a small amount of glue down the back of each envelope to page or project. Be sure they can spread open when filling with photos or other memorabilia.

materials

envelope(s) (or envelope template, page 140)
cardstock
decorative paper
printed tissue paper
inkjet transparencies
inkjet waterslide decals
stickers
metal alphabets
metal embellishments
printed ribbon
staples
absorbent ground medium
soft gel gloss medium
waxed twine
ink
adhesive
foam tape squares
shadow box

tools

alphabet and date stamps
needle tool
plastic envelope template system
pinking scissors
sponge dauber
paint brush
bone folder
scissors
paper trimmer

accordion pocket project idea:

snow fun shadow box collage

Displayed in a shadow box with interesting ephemera, photos, or other memorabilia, this pocket makes a lovely piece of art. Can't stop at just one? Try making a series of accordion pocket collections with themes such as the four seasons, summer vacations, or family reunions. For extra interest, this pocket holds three little transparent photo collages instead of standard photos.

instructions

To create the pocket, cut out envelopes, without the top flaps, using the envelope template shown on page 140 (or cut off the top flap of pre-made envelopes). Apply a small amount of glue down the back middle of each envelope. Place each envelope slightly higher than the one in front of it. Decorate the envelopes with decorative paper, ink, stickers, and inkjet waterslide decals of photos.

To create the transparent photo collages, print photos on transparencies and paint the main subject from behind with the absorbent ground medium. Cut a piece of cardstock to the same size as the transparency and collage it with paper, tissue, and stamps. Cut out desired photo mats and attach the transparencies, collaged cardstock, and mats together with ribbons, staples, and waxed twine. Decorate with stickers and metal embellishments set in soft gel gloss. Insert transparent photo collages into pockets using adhesive and foam tape squares to hold open the envelopes. Mount in a shadow box.

pullouts for images

Image elements to include in pullouts:

- *Groups of photos, such as a day at the park or a vacation*
- *Photos from loved ones in a memory book*
- *Photos with coordinating ephemera*
- *Photos documenting progress*

creating a
flip/flop pullout

This pullout is packed full of fun. It begs to be opened over and over. This is also one of those projects that looks difficult, but is easy. Tailor this book to hold forty great photos or twenty favorite Chinese fortunes. The possibilities are infinite!

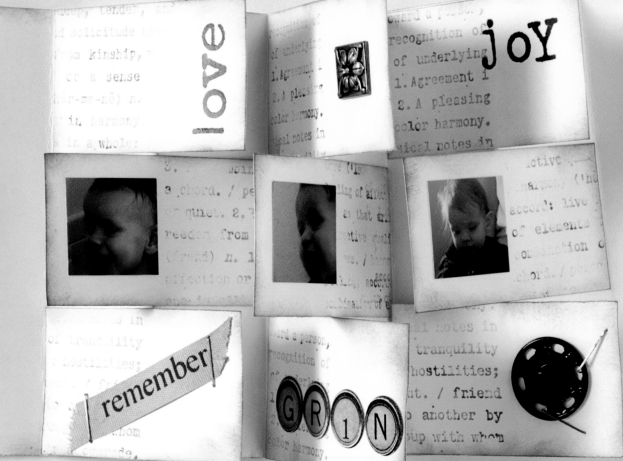

materials

cardstock

mat board

decorative paper

adhesive

removable double-sided tape

tools

bone folder

scissors

paper trimmer

instructions

This tool works by alternating pictures (or inserts) between the front and back facing panels of an accordion folded spine. In this example, the tool pictured here has nine inserts, three per accordion fold. Two of the inserts are attached to the front facing panel and one is attached to the back facing panel.

First, decide how many pictures (or inserts) are needed for the book and how big they will be. This will determine how many pleats are necessary.

Measuring on the longer side of the cardstock, cut it to fit the height of the pullout. Fold into an accordion (see Folding an Accordion, page 16). For a shorter accordion, it is easier to cut off panels after folding the entire sheet evenly. For a longer accordion, fold a second sheet of cardstock and overlap one panel from each accordion; secure with adhesive.

Plan the position of photos (or inserts) in the Flip/Flop Pullout using removable double-sided tape. Once positioning is finalized, adhere the photos.

Make book boards for the covers and glue accordion between them if desired (see Covering Book Boards, page 14). To tie the Flip/Flop Pullout shut with a ribbon, sandwich the ribbon between the back book board and the accordion before gluing together. Cut endpapers slightly smaller than book boards and glue to inside covers. Embellish the project as desired.

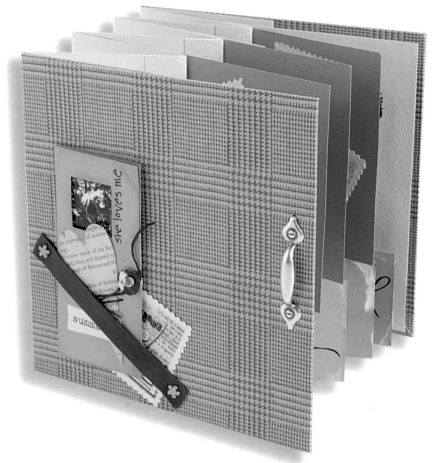

materials

mat board
cardstock
decorative paper
stickers
metal handle
old book pages
printed rubber band
waxed twine
decorative clips
paper tags
metal photo corners .
woven photo corners
brads
rub-ons
paper flowers
printed ribbon
staples
ink
acrylic paint
snap tape
foam tape squares
adhesive

tools

stapler
sponge dauber
circle and square punch
bone folder
sanding block or sand paper
scissors
paper trimmer

flip/flop pullout project idea:

she loves daddy memory book

It all starts with a few enticing embellishments on the book's cover—a metal handle, a section of rubber band, and an even smaller booklet of sugar-coated extras. Inside this Flip/Flop Pullout memory book, a mixture of large and small panels commemorates a brief moment in time when a little girl thought her daddy was the whole world. The embellishments inside all reinforce the feeling of a gentler time and a special love.

instructions

Cut and cover the front of two 6 ¼" (15.9 cm)-square mat boards (see Covering Book Boards, page 14).

Cut a piece of 12" × 12" (30.5 × 30.5 cm) cardstock in half. Accordion fold each sheet into four panels (see Folding an Accordion, page 16). Cut four 1 ½" × 6" (3.8 × 15.2 cm) strips of decorative paper, score, and fold them in half lengthwise. Attach the two folded accordions together by gluing one of the 1 ½" × 6" (3.8 × 15.2 cm) strips on top of the joint where the two accordions meet and one underneath the joint. The center of the accordion should be a mountain fold; use the other two strips for the adjoining mountain folds for a consistent decorative treatment.

Embellish the front cover with a handle, rubber band section, brads, and small tri-folded booklet made from scrap paper, photos, and embellishments.

Glue the first and last panels of the accordion to the inside of the book board covers. Glue endpapers cut slightly smaller than the covers.

Cut three large page inserts and three small inserts from cardstock. Add distressed photos (see Distressing Photos and Paper, page 17) and collage elements to the inserts. Alternate the inserts in the book. Attach large inserts to the top of the back panels of the accordion. Attach small inserts at the bottom of the front accordion panels. Secure with adhesive, and be sure to line them up evenly.

materials

cardstock

fasteners

reinforcements

extended eyelets

ball chain

ribbon

metal rings

tools

hole punch

scissors

paper trimmer

eyelet setting tools

If you just love holding a swatch book of paint chips in your hand and you have always wanted to use ball chain in your art, the swing pullout is the answer to your creative prayers! Hang an assortment of photos from a scrapbook page or tuck a ribbon-tied stack of travel photos into your collage. The swing pullout can stand on its own too! Collect photos of loved ones and favorite quotes to make a beautiful gift book.

instructions

Cut multiple pieces of same-sized cardstock and punch holes for fastening the pieces together. Use reinforcements or eyelets around each hole to minimize wear and tear.

You can use lightly fastened extended eyelets to hold a book together. Other options include fasteners, ball chain, ribbon, or metal rings to fit the feel of the project.

this place is a circus swing photo book

When there is a big story to tell, then the camera is mightier than the pen—and it's time to make a photo journal like this one. Attached with industrial-feeling ball chain and covered with a multitude of ribbon scraps, this Swing Pullout book has people "swinging" all over it. To further the theme of the project, the photos of a park day are enhanced by the use of pages from an old children's circus book. Bring in the clowns!

(continued on next page)

materials

cardstock
decorative paper
mat board
children's book pages
ribbons
ball chain with closure
ribbon charm
metal plaques
paper tags
rub-ons
waxed twine
decorative clips
adhesive
ink

tools

sponge dauber
sanding block or sand paper
craft knife
bone folder
hole punch
paper trimmer

(continued from previous page)

instructions

Cut and cover four mat board pages using book illustrations (see Covering Book Boards, page 14). Collage the photos onto the covered mat boards and add rub-ons, ribbon, waxed twine, and other embellishments (see photo, below). Punch hole in mat board with hole punch. Secure swing book pullout with ball chain. Tie scraps of ribbon to the chain, making sure to leave room so the book can swing open.

mini book pullout

There are so many ways to add mini books to a project; the ones presented here only scratch the surface. If you enjoy bookmaking, research techniques and adapt them to create a Mini Book. In the most basic sense, a book consists of a cover that encloses interior pages. How you put those together is up to you. Try any one of the binding tools on the market, or twist a spiraled piece of wire through punched holes. Use fibers to lace a book together or use colored staples for a quick pulled-together look.

materials

cardstock
waxed twine
binding spines

tools

paper clips
hole punches
binding tools
needle

instructions

Make a book cover (see Covering Book Boards, page 14).

Cut and/or fold paper to fit in between the covers.

Use paper clips or clamps to hold your book together while binding or attaching the cover to the interior pages. Punch holes for binding (or poke holes for sewing). To sew a binding, start at the top hole. Alternate straight stitches down the spine with a stitch around the spine at each hole using waxed twine or other sturdy fiber (center image). Get creative with binding methods; the options are limitless. For other book construction ideas see the Tag Book (page 31), Flip/Flop Pullout (page 71), Swing Pullout (page 74), and Dueling Accordions (page 112).

materials

cardstock
printed blue print tissue paper
screw binding posts
black twine
hardware fastener assortment
label holder
ink
glue stick

tools

alphabet and date stamps
scissors
hole punch
bone folder
needle tool
paper trimmer
eyelet setting tools

mini book pullout project idea:

home 2004 book

Inspired by a series of house construction pictures, this Mini Book Pullout is also a flip book! Flip from front to back to watch one side of the house being built; turn the book over and watch construction from the other side of the street. The embellishments for this book are hardware store items to fit the theme. Other possibilities for themes include a collection of maternity or school pictures, or even a book of mini collages.

instructions

Determine the number of pages desired for the mini book pullout and cut strips that measure 2" (5.1 cm) wide by the determined height of the pages. Score or fold each strip in half vertically to make it easier to open the book.

To create a book page, carefully glue two pictures back to back, sandwiching ½" (1.3 cm) of the strip between them. Create remaining pages in the same fashion. Line up all the pages and mark four holes with a needle tool through the spine. Punch four holes in each strip making sure the two outside holes will fit the screw binding posts. (The other two holes

are for the tie in the featured book.) Attach the book together using the binding posts and decorative washers. Add black twine and other hardware fasteners as desired.

To make the book sleeve, wrap a piece of cardstock around the book with just the binding showing. Use your fingers to press slight creases at the corners on the sides and bottoms.

Open the cardstock back up and layer with the printed tissue paper. Add label holder with stamped title and sharpen creases using a bone folder. Cut off the excess cardstock leaving some overlap and glue together to create the case.

hiding places for images

Ideas for elements to include in hiding places:

- *Pictorial timeline of important dates*
- *Ultrasound photos*
- *Photos of silly faces*
- *Important but less than perfect photos*

creating a
secret enclosure hiding place

materials
cardstock
embellishments
photos
ink
adhesive

tools
bone folder
craft knife
scissors
paper trimmer

This tool is a true hiding place. Like a secret door hidden behind a photo, this tool conceals its contents with minimal effort. The photo can be covertly cut down the middle, or be left whole and placed over tri-folded cardstock to conceal the secrets within just as effectively. This tool can easily be used as a card or be added to an altered book or a mini album.

instructions

Determine the height and width of the item you want to be the secret enclosure. Double the height or the width, depending on whether you want the hiding place to open vertically or horizontally, and cut a piece of cardstock to that size. Tentatively position the enclosure item on the cardstock, and fold in both sides to meet in the center (as short in the example at left), or off center (as shown above). Add a photo over the entire enclosure and attach to one side, or cut the photo and attach so that it opens with each side of the enclosure.

materials

cardstock
decorative paper
printed acetate
page tabs
rub-ons
square brads
cut down paint brush
needle and thread
leaves
cards
foam core
fluid acrylics
soft gel gloss medium
adhesive
black writing pen

tools

die-cut alphabets
paint brush
scissors
paper trimmer

secret enclosure hiding place project idea:

all boy, all ben scrapbook page

The Secret Enclosure Hiding Place is a natural choice for a scrapbook page. This page, a collection of pictures from different times of the year, tells a pictorial story of one little boy. Inside the secret enclosure could be silly photos, extra photos, or even a note about everything important that happened that year. Because this tool looks like a photo mat, it fits easily into any page without distracting from the overall design.

instructions

Create center shadow box for the left page (see Cutting Shadow Boxes, page 15). Insert a double-layer decorative paper mat, rub-on title, and ephemera (paint brush, leaves, cards, slips of paper, threaded needle) using soft gel gloss medium as an adhesive.

Cut eight small mats for the left page and a large cardstock mat for the right page. Lightly distress the mats and the top layer of the shadow box using a mixture of fluid acrylics and soft gel gloss.

Position the eight small mats on the left page. Overlay the printed acetate. Add page tab captions to each photo and layer onto the page with a second photo mat.

On the right page, make a secret enclosure hiding place with a tri-folded piece of card-stock. Layer this with a large photo embellished with strips of paper and brads as decorative corners. Attach to another mat before adhering to the large distressed mat and background paper. Trim outside edges of the page with four strips of decorative paper and square brads. Die cut the remainder of the title and adhere to page.

page flap hiding place

Buckles, snaps, and ribbons, oh my! This is a great way to hide those extra photos or close up little books for safekeeping. Make sure to reinforce closures so that they can withstand many openings and closings!

materials

cardstock

gold locks

swimsuit strap

brads

frog closure

tools

craft knife

scissors

paper trimmer

instructions

Choose a page size and determine the width of the flap. Add 1" extra (2.5 cm) to fold over and reinforce the flap edge. Use brads, eyelets, staples, or glue to adhere a closure to the page. Don't feel restricted to making a page flap on the side of a page; try adding one to the top or bottom instead.

page flap pullout project idea:

pilot's log

The perfect way to remember a special event or person is to create a memory book. Although this book looks complicated, the structure is easy to create using self-adhesive paper and some simple paper cuts. This book uses the page flap tool as an effective cover closure.

instructions

Cut six square pieces of mat board to desired book size. Cut six pieces of base cardstock color to the dimensions of mat board, adding 2" (5.1 cm) to the width.

Glue the first piece of cardstock to the first board; leave the excess paper hanging over the right side. Glue the overhang to the second board. Glue the next piece of cardstock to the same board, covering the flap from the previous board and letting the excess hang over the right side. Continue attaching the remaining boards in this fashion, except for the last board. On the last board, glue the cardstock leaving the overhang on the left side. This will be your page flap.

(continued on next page)

(continued on next page)

materials

cardstock
self-adhesive metal paper
metal quote stickers
stamps
metal photo corners
silver locks
suspender clips
ribbon
foam cushion
black writing pen
ink
foam tape
industrial strength tape
adhesive

tools

craft knife
scissors
paper trimmer
sewing machine

(continued from previous page)

To create the spine, cut a piece of cardstock to the width of the spine (measure the stacked edge of your covered mat board pages) and the height of the book. Adhere the spine in the middle a piece of self-adhesive paper (the metallic paper in the featured project) cut to desired dimension (4" [10.2 cm] wider than the spine works well). Adhere the paper carefully to the first board then fold the rest of the pages over to close the book. Adhere the remaining adhesive paper to the back cover.

Reinforce the side page flap from the back cover with a second piece of cardstock cut to the same dimensions as the overhang, adding 2"–3" (5.1–7.6 cm) to the width. Line up the cardstock with the overhang from the back of the book; glue the cardstock only to the back of the book. Make score lines in both pieces of cardstock to create the page flap so that it folds neatly around the pages.

To create the straps, fold a long strip of paper into thirds; use a sewing machine to stitch the trifolded strap along each edge. Cut the straps approximately 1" (2.5 cm) longer than the distance from the locks to the right side of the book. Mark the placement of the straps at the first crease in the page flap and carefully use a craft knife to cut a slit. Feed the straps through the hole and reinforce the hole with trimmed metal photo corners.

Decorate the inside pages as desired.

creating an
all-in-one hiding place

If you love paper engineering and interlocking cards, this is your hiding place! The hiding place is a card, insert, and envelope closure "all in one." You can make a very simple All-in-One Hiding Place that closes on itself like a cardboard box, or you can add visual interest with a few matching die cuts or large punches. After making a couple of these, you'll want to start experimenting with other fun ways to incorporate them into projects.

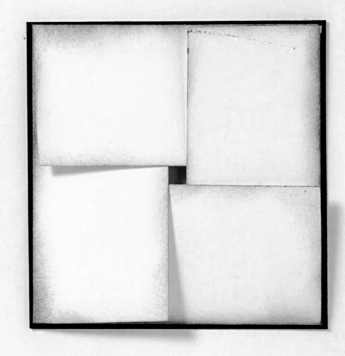

materials

cardstock

pencil

adhesive

tools

die cuts or large punches

bone folder

scissors

paper trimmer

instructions

For the square card (above right), cut a square of cardstock twice as big as you want the All-in-One Hiding Place to be. (For example, if the hiding place is 4" × 4" [10.2 × 10.2 cm], cut the cardstock to 8" × 8" [20.3 × 20.3 cm].) Score and fold in two of the cardstock sides to meet just short of the center of the card. Open the cardstock and fold in the opposite two sides. Unfold the cardstock again. Use scissors to cut out the square at each outside corner that is created by the fold lines. Fold the card in, one side at a time and moving clockwise around the square, tucking the last flap under the first (as you would secure the flaps of a cardboard box).

To make the interlocking All-in-One Hiding Place (above left), cut a strip of cardstock that is the same width and twice as long as the final card size. Score and fold the cardstock to meet at the center line. Choose two matching die cuts or large punch shapes and embellish as desired. Adhere one paper shape to the edge of each flap so that the shapes overlap.

Use a pencil to lightly mark cut lines. The cut lines are placed along the centerline where the shapes meet, on the right of one shape, and on the left half of the other. Use scissors to cut along the pencil lines. Decorate the hiding place as desired. Interlock the shapes to close.

materials

cardstock
jute
mica
glassine envelopes
tissue paper
inks
adhesive

tools

alphabet stamps
sponge dauber
scissors
paper trimmer

all-in-one hiding place project idea:

we're living out of boxes moving announcement

The familiar feel of a corrugated cardboard and stamping reminiscent of moving box markings strengthen the theme of this moving announcement. It's also "packed" with information. However, this card could be easily changed to be a picnic invitation by using red-and-white checked paper and sticker ants, a thank you card by using floral paper and ribbon corners, or a baby announcement using soft pastel striped paper and a diaper pin. The versatility of this all-in-one card makes it suitable for many applications.

instructions

Create a square All-in-One Hiding Place and ink the edges of the card to resemble wear. Stamp a rectangle of mica and glue to the "box" top. Stamp other words on box. Computer generate a message on a square card and on an address card. Slip address card into a glassine sleeve. Ink and layer the message card. Insert contents into the box with a small piece of crumpled tissue paper. Fold an interlock the flaps and tie with jute.

materials

journal
waxed linen
decorative paper
cardstock
button
markers
acrylic paint
glue stick

tools

scissors
paper trimmer
needle and thread

poppets in pockets journal (below right)

Claudine Hellmuth

This artist calls her collaged people "poppets." Here, they are safely tucked into the Accordion Pocket (see page 67) for safe keeping.

instructions

Glue decorative paper onto a journal page and paint with acrylic paint to soften the pattern. Create an Accordion Pocket (see page 67). Decorate the front of the pocket with images. Add photos to the pockets. Use a glue stick to adhere the pocket to the journal page. Sew a button to the front pocket. Attach waxed linen to the back pocket, winding the linen thread around the button to hold the pocket closed.

materials

cardstock
decorative paper
burlap
ribbon
pearls
label holder
sea shells
cigar box
transparency
paint (gel medium, fluid acrylics)
ink
adhesive

tools

stamps
heat tool
scissors
paper trimmer
paint brush

cigar box photo shrine (above left)

Jenna Beegle

This cigar box is the perfect shrine to capture special memories. Inside, the artist used a Catch-All Pocket (see page 64) to hold the special photos that can easily be removed for reminiscing.

instructions

Layer thin coats of different paints on the outside and front edges of the cigar box. Use the heat tool to distress and heat-impress designs around the inside of the box and the front edges. Tear edges of decorative paper and glue inside the box; distress edges with heat tool.

Fold a pocket from cardstock. Add a frayed piece of burlap to the front. Add ribbon and a stamped, distressed title in a label holder to the pocket. Glue the pocket into the box and add shells and pearls. Attach a transparency to the back of the box. Place photos in the pocket.

sunshine state scrapbook page

Katherine Brooks

The Lace-Up Pocket (see page 61) on this page holds extra surprises and complements a page filled with textural embellishments, images, and customized elements.

materials

stickers
patterned paper
cardstock
vellum
binding discs
rub-ons
brads
jute
netting
ribbon
staples
chip board
brown chalk ink
walnut ink
ink
paint
diamond glaze
adhesive
tag templates

tools

rubber stamps
"anywhere" hole punch
square punch
scissors
paper trimmer

instructions

To create the Lace-Up Pocket, cut two pieces of chipboard to desired size and cover with patterned paper. Sand and ink edges with brown chalk ink. Cut a window in one of the pieces. Stamp "Florida" and other images. Punch holes on each piece of the pocket.

Place pocket on layout. Punch holes on both sides and along the bottom with an "anywhere" hole punch. Adhere a photo behind the window of the pocket. Lace up the pocket with ribbon. Attach it with brads through the punched holes.

Use the square punch to punch photos out and adhere to two large walnut-inked tags. Machine stitch around the edges of photos. Finish tags with jute and tuck into the pocket. Finish the rest of the page as desired.

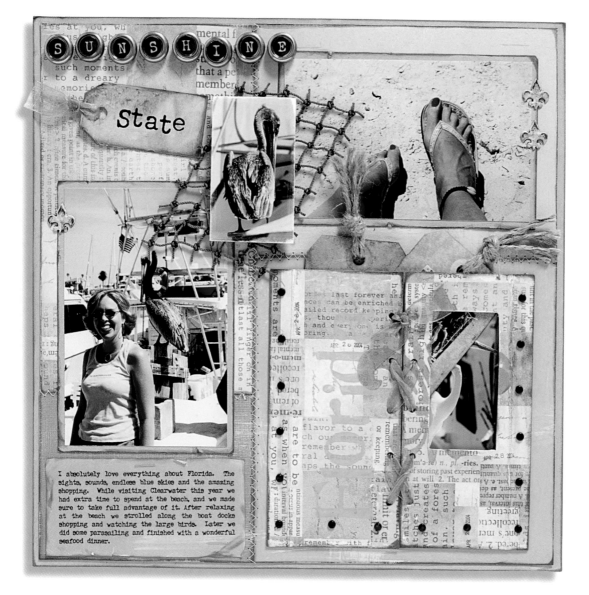

materials

chipboard
cardstock
patterned paper
photo turns
alphabets
conchos
ring fasteners
metal frames
eyelet letters
rub-ons
brads
foam tape squares
adhesive
ribbon
woven stickers
ink

tools

scissors
hole punch
paper trimmer

what makes us friends memory book

Rebecca Odom

As a tribute to a friend, the artist made this stand-alone Swing Pullout (see page 74) that can be put together with one or two ring clips.

instructions

Cut two pieces of chipboard to desired size for covers. Cover the outside with patterned paper and the inside with cardstock. Ink the edges.

Attach eyelet letters and ink to the cardstock for the front cover and adhere. Add title, frame, and picture to finish the cover. Punch hole(s).

Cut several pieces of cardstock slightly smaller than the cover. Punch hole(s) in the pages and ink the edges. Print text on pages. Add a strip of coordinating cardstock to each page, covering the seam with ribbon, a letter, and a concho. Add a photo and a photo turn for each page. Assemble the book by adding one or more rings.

wedding memory book

Jennifer Francis Bitto

In this Flip/Flop Pullout (see page 71), the artist layers elements that engage the senses to commemorate the special occasion of her wedding.

instructions

Cut two pieces of mat board for the book covers. Cover them using spray adhesive and gingham fabric (see Covering Book Boards, page 14). Fold black cardstock into accordion folds (Folding an Accordion, page 16) and attach the left panel to the front cover and the right panel to the back cover. Cut six tags from coordinating green cardstock and collage over them adding personal mementos and text. Glue tags to accordion folds as shown.

Add ribbon to front and back covers. Line the inside covers with patterned paper. Stamp sentiments with green ink. Glue photo with grosgrain ribbon corners to cover. Layer with printed twill and a scrap of grosgrain. Secure heart brad and attach to lower corner of cover. Add found acorns to the other ribbon corner with glue.

materials

fabric
mat board
photos
ribbon
printed twill tape
brads
acorns
cardstock
patterned paper
game pieces
table of contents from an old
  wedding book
postage stamp
reduced invitation
eyelets
envelope
dictionary text
oak leaf
tag
embossed acorns
heart clip
buttons
label
fork charm
printed ribbon
personalized postage stamp
adhesive
ink

tools

stamps
scissors
paper trimmer

materials

tags
labels
acetate
cardstock
frames
book paper
ribbon
cardboard
ephemera
diamond glaze
paint
walnut ink
adhesive
ink
tin mint box

tools

rubber stamps
scissors
paper trimmer
paint brush

enchantment scrapbook page

Stephanie McAtee

The artist has added an unorthodox Mini Book Pullout (see page 77) on this page along with vintage jewelry and other dimensional items for a unique and interactive scrapbook page.

instructions

Cut and fold cardboard to create a page with interactive doors. Add ephemera, paint, stamps, and other desired embellishments.

Use a stapled piece of acetate to hold a mini book (see page 77) on the page without interfering with the basic layout. Add photos and ephemera to the book and slide into the acetate sleeve.

To create an accordion journal strip, attach a tin mint box to the layout and add the journal using artisan labels as tabs. Add old book text to the tabs to write out a thought. Fold the entire page up and slide it into a page protector in a scrapbook.

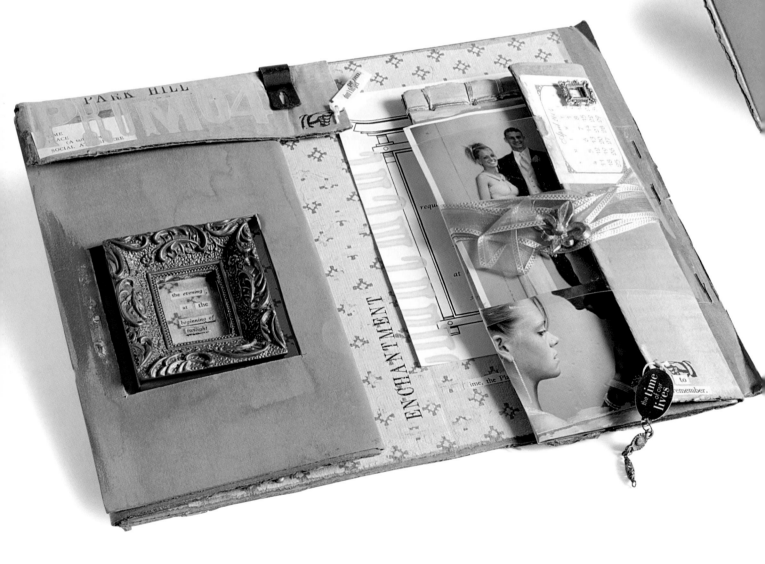

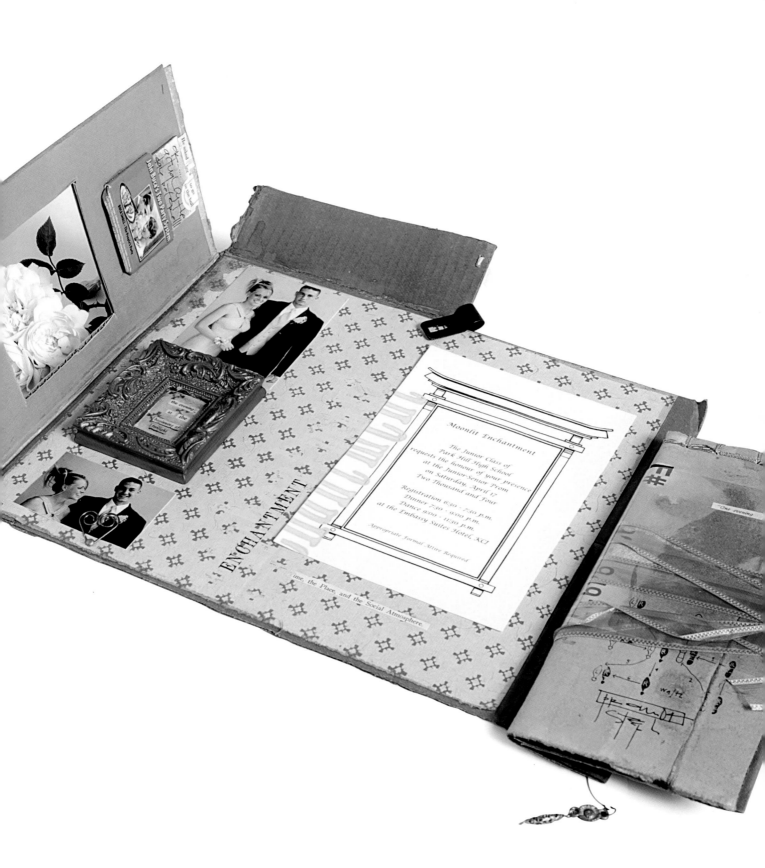

alice triptych

Suzi Finer

This creative triptych uses the Page Flap Hiding Place (see page 84) as a double closure to conceal a highly detailed and collaged mural.

materials

foam core
dried flowers
ribbon
T pins
decorative paper
mesh
dowel
coasters
fluid acrylics
soft gel medium
foam tape squares
diamond glaze
glue stick
photos

tools

craft knife
paint brushes
sand paper

instructions

Cut foam core to the desired sizes, making one board twice as wide as the two "door" panels. Paint the scene on the outside of the "door" panels. Attach the front panels to the main panels with hinges made of large paper strips cut to the height of the panels and adhered with soft gel medium. On inside panels, layer papers, coasters, and photos. Distress photos with sandpaper and then layer with textured papers, flowers, decorative paper, and touches of paint. Use scrap cardboard to paint additional characters and cut out with craft knife. Layer these characters on the board with foam tape squares.

To create the closure, fold small bits of ribbon in half and T-pin into the edge of the foam core on alternating sides, creating loops. Slide a painted dowel through all loops to hold the triptych closed.

materials

80# cover stock
medium and light weight vellum
80# text or 24# writing paper
PVC glue
vellum tape
removable double-sided tape

tools

craft knife
scoring tool
ruler
scissors

if using the seven-hole pamphlet stitching
Bookbinders awl
blunt tapestry needle
linen thread (or something similar)

wedding memory book

Marta Simmons-Wiechmann

The artist has created a series of interactive Secret Enclosure Hiding Places (see page 81) to commemorate her wedding. The cards can be kept individually or be sewn into a book binding.

instructions

To create the card, determine final desired size; double the measurement and add 1/4" (0.6 cm) to the width; cut from cover stock. Score two lines, each one half the width of the card plus 1/8" (0.3 cm) away from either end of the cover stock. Fold sides in toward the center; the edges will overlap in the middle.

Scan and print a collection of photos onto lightweight vellum and attach to the back of the card with vellum tape.

For the fly sheet, cut medium weight vellum the length of the base card and 1 1/2 times the width, minus 1/8" (0.3 cm). Score and fold vellum so that the front is twice as wide as the back.

For the signature, cut the text paper the same width and length as your base card. Score in half and fold. Place as many signatures as desired, but cut the ends flush if necessary. Place the signature inside the fly sheet, and then place this inside the left side of base card. Align top and bottom and stitch (this artist chose the seven-hole pamphlet technique) to join the pieces.

Decorate the front of the card and repeat with as many cards as desired. All cards seen here are sewn into a book binding. To keep cards closed, try using removable double-stick tape.

mexico scrapbook page

Rhonda Solomon

The sunny All-in-One Hiding Place (see page 87) on this page complements the graphically decorated title "Mexico."

materials

cardstock
decorative papers
stickers
button
twine
ribbon
negative sheet protector
wire screen
acrylic paint
paint swatches
embossing powders
adhesive
ink

tools

hand sewing needle
stamps
sewing machine
scissors
paper trimmer
paint brush

instructions

Paint wire screen with paint, cut a hole from the center to fit photo, and stitch to leather paper with twine. Fill a negative sheet. Create a title for one of the squares using stamps. Gather paint swatches, inks, embossing powders, and other embellishments to fill the other squares, then stitch the sheet to the background page.

Make an All-in-One Hiding Place by cutting corrugated paper to desired size. Score and fold the paper and zigzag stitch a sun on each flap so they overlap when closed. Cut half way in from the top of one sun and halfway in from the bottom of the other. Add photos and text inside the hiding place. Interlock suns to close and attach to the layout. Stamp images in the layout background and add ribbon.

chapter 4 using ephemera

Many artists are guilty of collecting all things sentimental—items such as fortune cookie fortunes, movie stubs, and love notes scribbled on sticky notes. They often find themselves collecting tidbits of ephemera specifically for art. Flea markets become thrilling. An invitation to pore over an old trunk from a loved one's attic is almost too much to bear. I am the sentimental type. I like to keep everything, from a lock from my daughter's first haircut to the train tickets from my grandmother's teenage travel.

It's important to find the balance between preserving actual items and finding ways to include these one-of-a-kind items in artwork. Color copying, using de-acidification spray, enclosing or adding paper buffers to precious items are all ways to add these items to a project safely. In this chapter, learn about the tools that make it possible to incorporate these wonderful items with ease.

pockets for ephemera

Ideas for elements to include in pockets:

- *Photocopies of bulky keepsakes*
- *Pressed leaves and flowers*
- *Nature walk collections*
- *Paper napkins or matchbook souvenirs*
- *Invitations*
- *Old school supplies*
- *Baby hospital band*

creating a
slash pocket

When using large or bulky items in your work, the slash pocket can be employed well. Make it tall and skinny, short and wide, or square to fit the item. Use several pockets together and bind them along one edge to make a keepsake book, or make paper hinges to attach the slash pockets into an accordion.

materials
cardstock
adhesives

tools
scissors
paper trimmer
bone folder

instructions

Determine the desired height and width of the Slash Pocket. Cut a piece of cardstock twice the width plus ½" (1.3 cm), and the desired height plus ½" (1.3 cm).

Score a fold line ½" (1.3 cm) from one side and along the bottom of the pocket; these are the tabs for the pocket. Fold in along the score lines. Fold the pocket in half, aligning the unscored side with the score line, but don't adhere yet.

Trim the top angle of the pocket on the front half the cardstock (the front side with both tabs). Trim off the excess tab from the back half of the pocket and cut the remaining tabs on the diagonal. Use glue or double-stick tape to secure the tabs and create the pocket.

Note: The Slash Pocket template on page 143 will accommodate a CD or DVD perfectly.

slash pocket project idea:

discover time scrapbook layout

When designing a page, think about including a CD or a DVD appropriate for the page; the recorded voice of a toddler, calming sounds of nature, a special collection of digital photos, or a video. Include other three-dimensional items and repeat the use of circles to reinforce the design.

instructions

Create Slash Pocket using the template on page 143. Stamp and title the pocket before closing it (see lower right corner of page layout). Insert a coordinating mat inside the pocket and add CD or DVD. Make a game board spinner from store-bought,

materials

cardstock
game board spinner or arrow
raffia
overall buckles
brads
safety pin
vellum
adhesive
black embossing powder
black writing pen
black permanent marker
ink
template (see page 143)

tools

stamps
scissors
paper trimmer
craft knife
inkjet printer

There are times when I'm watching you and grandpa and I feel as though I'm not even there. Like a butterfly flitting about, I watch you. You absorb everything grandpa has to say or show you. I sneak a picture of you to help me remember how small you once were and to help you remember how much grandpa loves you. I hope you always share your sense of wonder with me and grandpa.

pre-cut shapes, or make your own from simple arrow shapes or clock-making supplies. Secure it with a brad.

Add colored cardstock mats with strips of torn vellum to photos. Add overall buckles to focal photo. Make faux overall straps with the extra paper. Draw in stitch lines on the straps, insert them into the buckles, and adhere them to the page over background blocks of color.

To journal, print onto vellum using an inkjet printer and apply black embossing powder to the ink while still wet; melt the powder. Cut out and adhere it to colored mats using vellum adhesive.

Create mini titles to place around the spinner using hand-cut or punched tags and strips of paper. Adhere photos to the page and add the mini titles with brads, raffia, and a safety pin. Add a hand-drawn or a computer-generated title and the remaining page elements.

creating a
plastic sleeve pocket

Try these plastic sleeves when a project calls for ephemera that can be easily seen and accessed. For long narrow pockets use negative holders; use sticker organizer sheets for small items such as coins or subway tokens.

materials

plastic sleeves

adhesive or attachments (thread, wire, brads eyelets, staples, pins, or paper clips)

tools

scissors

instructions

Find the appropriately shaped sleeve for the items to display. Cut desired number of sleeves from the main sheet, making sure to leave a little extra space to secure the sheet to the background.

For contrast, hide adhesive behind the ephemera or behind small mats that are inserted in the plastic sleeve behind the ephemera. Alternate ways of attaching the plastic sleeve pocket to projects by sewing, stapling, pinning, or paper clipping.

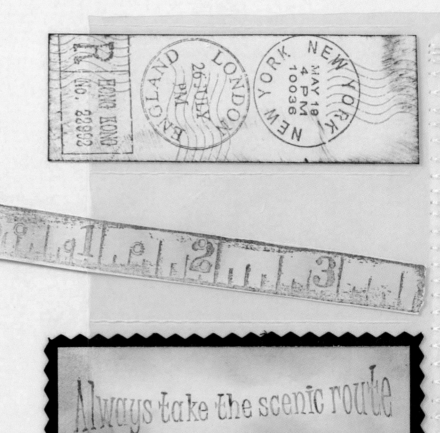

plastic sleeve project idea:

treasured memories

It's great to have a scrapbook page of a great vacation, but sometimes there are moments that deserve a little more attention. Here, a day at the beach and an inside look into the soul of two siblings are showcased in this treasure box and enclosed memory book. There are several do-it-yourself binding options, or have the work bound at a copy or office supply store. Instead of using actual ephemera or memorabilia that is fragile, color copy or scan and print the piece to preserve it or reduce bulk.

instructions

Paint base coat using two coordinating colors on the inside and outside of the paper chest; let dry. Stamp the chest randomly with different colored inks. Add stickers and rub edges with ink to age the chest.

Cut multiple mat boards ½" (1.3 cm) narrower than the inside width of the chest, and ⅝" (1.6 cm) shorter than the inside height of the chest. Lightly sponge two acrylic paint colors on the backs of the boards and let dry. Bind all of the boards together to create one long book using the binding machine and comb.

(continued on next page)

materials

plastic sleeve protectors
papier-mâché chest
cardstock
mat board with black core
printed paper
stickers
textured paint chips
fiber
square acrylic page bubbles
cardboard stencils
charms
markers
acrylic paint
inks, solvent- and dye-based
adhesive
foam square adhesive

tools

stamps
sponge daubers
paint brush
sea sponge
binding machine
binding comb
craft knife
scissors
paper trimmer
sand paper

(continued from previous page)

Crop and mount the photos as desired. Place the clear acrylic square bubbles over the decorative paper and cut them in half to create one-of-a-kind photo corners. To add interest to the photos, lightly sand the edges.

Distress stencil letters with ink and stamp them to add texture. Lightly age the brass charms with solvent-based inks. Tie them with the fibers and the charms and attach to the page over the paint chips with foam squares.

Write the names or message along the side of the paper chip with a marker.

Cut individual plastic sleeves from a plastic sleeve protector sheet. Age the sleeves with solvent-based inks. Stamp paint chips for inserts for the plastic sleeve pockets and add a color-copied ephemera on a foam square. Adhere the sleeve. Fold book and tuck it safely into the paper chest.

These pockets are the latest trend in show and tell! Show off travel ephemera and life's memorabilia in these little pockets made from clear plastic page protectors, or use purchased clear envelopes (see Sealed Envelope Hiding Place, page 41). These wonderful little gems are easily customized to fit a specific item perfectly! Get creative with your method of attachment: use twine, photo corners, staples, fasteners, brads, or eyelets. Use a heat tool to melt the pocket closed as in this project, or try sewing or other creative fastening methods.

materials

plastic page protectors

metal ruler or metal cookie cutter

ephemera

tools

heat tool with pointed tip

glass cutting mat

instructions

Warm a heat tool while assembling your ephemera. Sandwich ephemera between two sides of a plastic page protector. Place either a metal cookie cutter or metal ruler along ephemera; slowly and steadily trace around the items with the heat tool to melt and to seal the pocket. Note: Be sure to work over a glass cutting mat when using a heat tool.

materials

mat board
decorative paper
eyelets
woven stickers
stickers
jute
laser-cut surf board
printed acetate
page protector
miscellaneous beads
photographs

tools

scissors
paper trimmer
eyelet setting tools
heat tool with point tip
metal ruler
glass mat
hole punch

I can see clearly pocket project idea:

wish you were here travel folio

Here, the light, airy feel of the shore is captured in the pocket strung up in the middle. A wooden surfboard and some printed acetate give a real vacation memorabilia feel. When presented this way, collecting souvenirs takes on a whole new meaning. For a more feminine look, use ribbon instead of jute and more delicate eyelets. For a more artistic collage, mix and match eyelets and vary the ties throughout the folio.

instructions

Cut and cover four mat boards (see Covering Book Boards, page 14). Decorate the four boards with photos and stickers. Punch holes and set eyelets in all four corners of each board. Sandwich stickers, acetate, and laser-cut surfboard between two pieces of page protector and seal to create pocket (see I Can See Clearly Pocket, page 109). Add an eyelet to each corner of pocket. Use jute to tie the folio together and finish the ends with miscellaneous beads.

pullouts for ephemera

Ideas for elements to include in pullouts:

- *Chinese fortunes*
- *Flat collections*
- *A lock of hair*
- *Saved movie tickets*
- *Mini luggage tags*

dueling accordion pullout

To add some paper engineering pizzazz to a project, try this Dueling Accordion Pullout. Sandwich it between two pages to make the pages pop, or turn it into a self-standing book. Add timelines from your family history, detail a trip, journal school age years in each panel, or add a map from an important journey.

materials

cardstock

ink

tools

stamps

scissors

paper trimmer

bone folder

craft knife

instructions

Accordion fold two identical pieces of cardstock, making sure to fold them so that the artwork side is showing (see Folding an Accordion, page 16). To interlock the two accordions, make slits half the height of each accordion; start at the top of one and the bottom of the other. Feel free to experiment with the placement of these slits (they can be centered as shown here, or placed off-center for an exaggerated look), and with changing the heights of the dueling accordions for a unique look, as shown in this example.

dueling accordion pullout project idea:

the perfect journey memory book

The Dueling Accordion Pullout makes a great memory book, so it's a perfect form for commemorating a special trip. With lots of nooks and crannies, a book like this one can be customized to show the extreme sport of helicopter skiing, or even a tamer event, such as a chess match.

instructions

To create the large Dueling Accordion, cut two pieces of cardstock 8" × 12" (20.3 × 30.5 cm) and accordion fold into four 3" (7.6 cm) panels (see Folding an Accordion, page 16).

Make Dueling Accordion (see page 112); make slits 4" (10.2 cm) long, starting 1/2" (1.3 cm) from each fold and each end. Interlace these two accordion pieces by aligning slits and sliding together.

To create the small Dueling Accordion, cut two pieces of cardstock 2 1/2" × 12" (6.4 cm × 30.5 cm) and adhere ephemera, maps, photos, or time line as desired. Accordion fold into eight 1 1/2" (3.8 cm) panels; make sure to fold one piece of cardstock with the photo or ephemera showing on the inside and one with the photo or ephemera showing on the outside.

(continued on next page)

materials

cardstock
cardboard
maps
clear tags
rivets
stencils
frame
conchos
waxed fibers
alphabet charms
photo flips
paper tags
washer words
label holders
ink
black gesso
fluid acrylics
foam tape squares
industrial strength tape
photos

tools

scissors
hole punch
needle tool
black writing pen
bone folder
paper trimmer
sanding blocks or sand paper

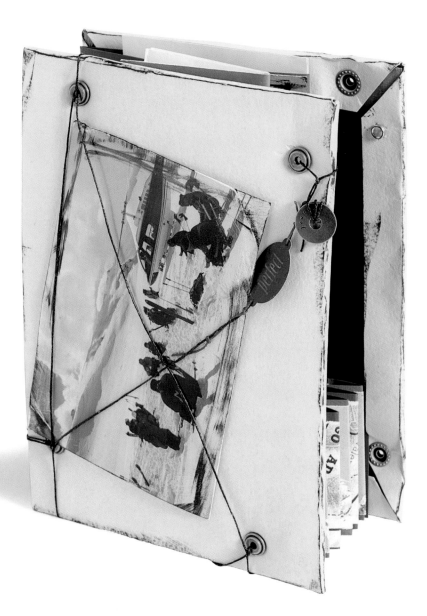

(continued from previous page)

Half way between each fold (including the ends), make slits 1 ¼" (3.2 cm) long and interlace these two accordion pieces by aligning slits and sliding together.

Embellish both Dueling Accordions with distressed photos and other attachments using adhesive, foam tape squares, and waxed twine. (Note: Some attachments might need to be put in place before interlacing the dueling accordions.)

For the cover, cut two pieces of 6" × 8" (15.2 × 20.3 cm) cardboard and randomly paint one side of each with black gesso and red acrylic; let dry. Cut two pieces of cardstock slightly larger than the cardboard to wrap the unpainted side of the cardboard covers. Fold excess cardstock around the cardboard pieces and miter the corners; secure them down with rivets and conchos. Reinforce with industrial double-stick tape where necessary. Age the edges with black ink. Attach covers to the first and last panels of the Dueling Accordions with industrial double-stick tape. Add extra ephemera to the cover with waxed twine and embellishments.

creating a
laminated tag pullout

materials

ephemera

luggage tags or lamination material

tools

hole punch

scissors

To display flat (or mostly flat) ephemera, use these fun laminated pullouts. Use ribbon, rubber bands, wire, or fibers to make these laminated tags easy to pull out of pockets or to hang from projects.

instructions

Use self-adhesive luggage tags, no-heat lamination materials, or heat-activated lamination material to laminate your ephemera. If you are using a laminating machine, remember to make sure that items will fit through the rollers. Follow the manufacturer's directions for the chosen lamination process and make tags. Trim the laminated item to chosen shape and size. Punch a hole, if needed, and add a pull tie.

materials

cardstock
vellum
patterned paper
reduced copies of certificates
brads
laminating tags
ink, solvent-based
ball chain
mat board
reflective letter
twill tape
adhesive
vellum adhesive
clear embossing powder

tools

craft knife
sponge
stamps
scissors
paper trimmer

laminated tag pullout project idea:

daisy's memory scrapbook page

When creating artwork, don't forget about the color copier! This fabulous machine can take large, valuable documents and make small, realistic copies. Use copies of bulky items instead of the originals. This page uses laminated pullouts as a hanging embellishment, but the pullouts could just as easily have been tucked into a pocket. There are some great laminating supplies on the market to experiment with. Important note: Make sure ephemera items are heat tolerant if you are using a heat lamination process.

instructions

Cut a mat board to a size slightly smaller than your layout and cut out the desired openings for the main photo and for the lower left shadow box (see Cutting Shadow Boxes, page 15). Glue the patterned paper to the cardstock (both the same size as your layout) around the outside edge and glue it to the mat board. Make a slit in the paper showing through the big opening and tear away the excess paper, separating the two layers. Glue the picture to the page from behind.

Print the journaling on the vellum and emboss it with ultrafine embossing powder. Add ink to the reflective letter and glue to the journaling. Use vellum adhesive to attach the journaling to the page.

Cut out a hole in the paper showing through the smaller opening and insert ephemera (the dog bone charm in this example). Cover the back of the opening with a coordinating cardstock.

Stamp the twill tape and attach to the page with glue on the backside. Make the laminated tags with reduced-sized color copies and laminating supplies and trim to the desired size. Age the tags with a solvent-based inkpad and a sponge. Attach the tags to the twill tape and secure with a decorative brad, using the brad legs to gather the twill tape together.

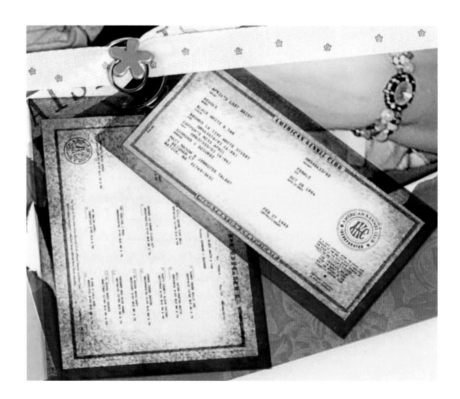

D

In Memory of
Daisy Mason
Beloved Companion

The size of Daisy's bark was only surpassed by her love for children. If dogs get to pick their heaven, then she is surrounded by laughing children who are licking ice cream cones. She is licking off the cold drips as they fall on the toes of the children, only to make them giggle more.

Daisy was also one of the finest hide-n-seekers I've ever known. Thanks for your company, Daisy. We miss you.

DAISY DAISY DAISY DAISY DAISY

OCT 1994 • MAR 2003

creating a
tag pouch pullout

Sometimes, there is a fine line between pockets and pullouts. This Tag Pouch Pullout is actually a string of pockets that together make a pullout (or one big pocket!) Fold a tag pouch up, add board book covers (see page 14) and a ribbon to create a fun little keepsake book. Try slipping a tag pouch into any of the pockets in this book, or tie it to a project with ribbon, fiber, or wire. As an alternative to folding, try sewing on the pouch (see Sharon Soneff's project, page 134).

materials

cardstock

decorative paper

fasteners or adhesive

tools

bone folder

hole and circle punches

scissors

paper trimmer

instructions

Determine the size of each individual panel and the depth of the pouch. Decide how many panels to include in the tag pouch; this is the panel number. Cut a piece of cardstock the width of an individual panel multiplied by the panel number. The height of your cardstock should be cut to the height of the individual panel plus the depth of the pouch.

Measure the depth of the pouch from the bottom of the cardstock; score and fold this line along the width of the cardstock. Score each line from top to bottom to mark each panel. Carefully fold back and forth along each line. Fold up the tag pouch completely, then cut off both top corners diagonally to create the tag shape.

Open up the Tag Pouch Pullout; punch circles from paper to serve as reinforcements for each tag's hole. Adhere these to the tag and punch a hole out of the center of each one. Use adhesives or fasteners to secure the outside edges of the pouch.

tag pouch pullout project idea:

reasons why I love you and wedding ensemble

These two Tag Pouch Pullout cards are the perfect example of taking a tool and using it in distinct ways. The pouch offers the perfect way to list reasons for loving someone; once your affections are returned, it's time for the wedding invitations. Daisies and leaf shapes are combined in this contemporary card with acetate-printed inserts. But, don't stop there—carry the theme throughout the wedding with items like a tag pouch menu!

instructions

For the Reasons Why I Love You Tag Pouch Pullout, cut out and score a tag pouch from a sheet of white paper. Ink the edges and fold up the pouch; secure with die cut silver tape hinges and brads. Computer generate text on white paper, cut out, and stamp (see photo on next page). Add label holder cut from silver tape on text paper. Attach vellum with brads and add a die-cut number. Mount each reason on a cardstock mat and insert into the pouches. Punch circles out of cardstock and glue them to the tops of the panels, then punch holes in their centers and trim.

(continued on next page)

(continued on next page)

materials

cardstock
vellum
printable acetate
handmade paper
text weight paper
silver metal tape
brads
fibers
ribbon
ink
absorbent ground medium
acrylic paint

tools

label holder, alphabet, number, and hinge die cuts
circle, seal, and daisy punches
heart and daisy stamp
paint brush
sponge dauber
sanding block
bone folder
scissors
paper trimmer
computer and printer

You are my biggest cheerleader and you believe I can do anything.

You love our girls with all your heart and you enjoy being wrapped around their little fingers.

You make me laugh even when I feel like crying.

You are strong when I am weak... ...you share my burdens and my joys.

Why I Love You

(continued from previous page)

Cut out a tag and die cut the letters to spell "reason" and glue to the tag. Cover the tag with the silver tape and press down around the letters with a bone folder to emboss. Color the tag with black and red permanent ink; use a fine sanding block to sand off the color, leaving a brushed metal surface with a hint of color in the crevices. Cover the back of the tag with cardstock and tie to the card with fibers.

To create the invitation, create a red tag pouch pullout and secure with punched reinforcements and daisies punched from handmade paper. Distress the edges with absorbent ground medium. Stamp daisies randomly around the pouch. Cut out large leaves from vellum and emboss vein patterns with a bone folder on a slightly firm surface; glue into the pouches. Computer generate a three-part invitation with a daisy clip art at the top. Paint edges of the transparencies and the daisies from behind with absorbent ground to make them pop. Tie closed with ribbon stamped with absorbent ground. Make the menu the same way as the individual tag pouch pullout, but create only one panel. Use a large piece of vellum in place of the large leaf, and tie small leaves from the top of the acetate with ribbon.

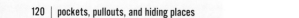

Menu

SPRING GREENS VINAGRETTE

CHILLED PENNE GORGONZOLA

FRUITED CHICKEN SALAD

FRESH ROLL SELECT

LEMON CHIFFON CAKE W

MINT JULEP AND LE

AMANDA MARIE
AND BRETT WARD,
WILL BE EXHANGING VOWS IN A
PRIVATE WEDDING CEREMONY
ON FRIDAY,
THE SECOND OF JULY

YOU ARE JOYFULLY INVITED
TO A WEDDING CELEBRATION
ON SATURDAY,
THE THIRD OF JULY
AT THE HOME OF
MR. AND MRS. ROBERT TALBOT

LOVE ISN'T LOVE 'TIL YOU
GIVE IT AWAY . . .
R.S.V.P.
BWNAT@AOL.COM
BY JUNE 20TH

hiding places for ephemera

Ideas for elements to include in hiding places:

- *Feathers*
- *Shells*
- *Secret treasures*
- *Lottery tickets*
- *Baby teeth*
- *Hidden collages*
- *Jewelry*
- *Lucky Charms*

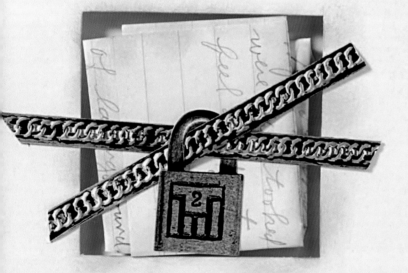

creating a
lock and key hiding place

materials

cardstock

foam core

locks or lock stickers

ribbons

fiber

metal strips

hinges and hardware

tools

craft knife or heat tool
with blade attachment

glass cutting mat

scissors

paper trimmer

This hiding place is perfect for keeping skeletons in the closet or guarding Fort Knox gold. So many things are suited to safekeeping! Do you keep your heart under lock and key? What about diary transcripts? This hiding place also offers a great use for those tiny luggage locks.

instructions

Cut a shadow box and cardstock to fit ephemera (see page 15). Use eyelets and brads to attach hinges and hardware to create a locking enclosure for the shadow box (see above right). Or, for a less dimensional treatment, use self-adhesive metal strips (above left) and run them through a lock sticker. Don't forget to put the key or code nearby!

To see an example using ribbon, see page 15.

lock and key hiding place project idea:

two by two memory book

Two sweet girls deserve nothing less than a life full of precious memories, and this little memory box is a wonderful way to start them off. Any number of things can go inside the hiding place: would it be hospital bracelets, the first lock of hair, or a note of love from Mom and Dad? Start a tradition by giving the gift of memories!

instructions

Cover two boards (see page 14) and cut a narrow spine from mat board, approximately ³/₄" (2 cm) wide by the height of the boards. Attach spine to the boards with decorative paper that overlaps the front of both boards. Cut an end paper slightly smaller than the cover and glue it inside, sandwiching in ribbons on both sides for a closure. For the cover, layer stickers and title using foam tape squares and ribbon where necessary.

(continued on next page)

materials

cardstock
foam core
decorative paper
mat board
rolled cork
stickers
ribbon
decorative brads
metal embellishments
paper flowers
tassel
lock and key
metal hardware
small box
ink
adhesive
foam tape squares
photographs

tools

alphabet and fleur-de-lis die cuts
bone folder
sponge dauber
sanding block or sand paper
scissors
paper trimmer

(continued from previous page)

For the left page, distress photos and layer two of them on torn cork; add metal embellishments and then adhere them all. Embellish the page with stickers, distressed paper flowers, and foam tape squares for dimension.

For the right page, create a shadow box from thick foam core or use two layers of thinner foam core. Distress paper with ink and wrap around foam core to cover the shadow box frame. Add the lock and hardware to the box. Attach the shadow box and box insert to the page. Use a decorative brad to poke a tassel and key into the foam core.

creating a
window box hiding place

materials

cardstock

foam core

acetate or vellum

adhesive

ephemera

tools

craft knife or
heat tool with
blade attachment

glass cutting mat

scissors

paper trimmer

This Window Box Hiding Place can hold flowers, coins, feathers, stamps, and other nostalgic ephemera. A simple shadow box base with acetate sandwiched in between can create a window to the soul! Try using vellum instead of acetate for a cloudy look; use printed or stamped acetate for a more complex look (see above right).

instructions

Cut cardstock and a shadow box from foam core to fit ephemera (see page 15). Insert ephemera to the shadow box foam core. Adhere acetate to cover the item, then complete the shadow box with the cardstock cover layer.

old book
vellum
stickers
feathers
brads
tags
printed ribbon
acetate
fiber
ribbon
adhesive
ink
soft gel gloss
ephemera
photographs

tools

craft knife
cutting mat
metal ruler
needle tool
scissors

window box hiding place project idea:

estes park memories altered book

Many times, books are altered for the sake of art; sometimes they are little journeys into special memories of families and travels, or hopes and dreams. This little book is a study in a special place and time and the accompanying feelings. Ephemera, photos, and collage are safely tucked behind a window box hiding place like a framed piece of art. Keep an eye out at flea markets for books to showcase special journeys!

instructions

Open book to the desired location for the embellishments. Bend up bottom corners of the previous few pages and secure with a brad. Bend additional pages before that up in the opposite direction as desired. Use adhesive along the edges of these two bunches of pages to form pockets. Secure with a brad. Skip two pages and then start gluing around the edge of each the next twelve to twenty pages. Slip a cutting surface under the last glued page. Carefully cut a window niche out of the first two unglued pages and the rest of the glued pages using a sharp craft knife and a metal ruler.

With the two unglued pages turned out of the way, collage the window niche with vellum, torn pages, ephemera, and photos; tuck bits and pieces into the different pages using soft gel gloss as an adhesive. Sandwich a piece of acetate just under the top unglued page and finish gluing down the top pages. Add a sticker and ribbon secured with brads. Ink to age as desired. Distress two tags and add stickers and fibers before tucking into the left pocket.

creating a
rolled-up hiding place

materials

fiber

wire

embellishment
strips or paper
scraps

adhesive

ephemera

This tool is fun, offering interesting new options for attaching maps and other rollable ephemera. Whether including memorabilia for its style or for sentimental reasons, this hiding place offers bold dimension. Use favorite fibers, wire, embellishment strips, or paper scraps to help hold cherished ephemera to the background.

tools

needle tool

craft knife

paper trimmer

instructions

Select ephemera that can be rolled and trim them to size. Use a needle tool to poke holes into the project for lacing, if desired. Other options for attaching these ephemera rolls include strips of decorative tape, cut strips of paper, or embellishments, wire, and fiber. Choose an option that fits the theme and will adequately support the weight of the ephemera.

rolled-up hiding place project idea:

seashell from the seashore shadow box collage

This sea-themed shadow box seems as though it was lifted right out of an archeologist's pack. Specimen tags, a Rolled-Up Hiding Place map, shells, and other ephemera take special trip mementos and transform them into art. When collecting pebbles on a walk or shells on the beach, consider using them in a project to highlight their beauty.

instructions

Paint the outside of the shadow box with a loose mixture of soft gel gloss and fluid acrylics. Cover the inside with strips of crumpled and distressed paper (see Distressing Photos and Paper, page 17). Cut a piece of foam core to fit snugly inside the frame; cover with distressed paper. Layer with a smaller piece of foam core and vellum paper.

To create the hiding place, roll up a map and secure it to a tall, narrow, rectangular piece of foam core painted with a mixture of absorbent and acrylic ground mediums and fluid acrylics; wrap with a strip of paper and fine brass wire. Add a small hanging frame box filled with a painted stencil and seahorse. Attach this assemblage to the right side of the vellum-covered foam core. Add shells, starfish, tags, stamped images, and rub-ons. Finish the shadow box with plastic letters painted with acrylic ground medium and rubbed with ink.

materials

cardstock
vellum
decorative paper
black foam core
map
hanging frame
stencil
seahorse
rub-ons
wire
raffia
tags
seashells
shadow box frame
plastic letters
round tags
inks
acrylic ground medium
absorbent ground medium
fluid acrylics
soft gel gloss

tools

stamps
scissors
paper trimmer
paint brushes
craft knife or heat tool with knife tip
metal ruler
cutting mat

materials

joss paper
tissue paper
rice paper
linen
organza
silk
mesh
inkjet transparencies
pressed flowers (or flower stickers)
canvas board
gold interference paint
acrylic paint
soft gel
gold spray paint
adhesive
ink

tools

stamp
sewing machine
scissors
paint brush
computer and printer

clear pocket collage

Christine Adolph

This fresh and flowery collage features an innovative use of acrylics, fabrics, and stamping. It is highlighted with soft printed transparencies and an I Can See Clearly Pocket (see page 109) that is holding a pressed flower.

instructions

Create a collage on a sheet of rice paper. Using soft gel, layer the left side of the rice paper with joss paper, tissue paper, organza, and silk painted with gold interference paint. Layer the right side with linen. Cut a heart out of a strip of organza and adhere to the collage, centering it in the joss paper. Add mesh to the collage. Stamp the dandelion and paint flowers. Spray gold paint over a pressed flower to create a silhouette. Print out photos and text on transparencies; stitch them to the collage with the pressed flower under one transparency. Finish embellishing with machine stitching and the butterfly stamp. Stabilize the collage onto canvas board or foam core and frame if desired.

candy bar picks scrapbook page

Darcee Thompson

These Plastic Sleeve Pockets (see page 106) help the artist tell her story and artfully hold her embellishments on this scrapbook page.

instructions

Cover a sheet of cardstock with clear embossing ink followed by powder, then melt with embossing gun. Repeat three times. Use heat tool with pen tip to draw lines creating grooves into the embossing powder. Use a paint brush to add pearlescent powders into the grooves and heat again with embossing gun. Use the heat tool again to make more texture lines. Cut out and adhere to the page with adhesive.

For the pockets, cut a baseball card holder pocket from a protector and fill with memorabilia and journaling. Layer the pocket over the frame and machine stitch around the edges on to the page. Write the journaling on vellum with the top and bottom torn. Chalk two pieces on the back and edge the torn edges with a darker marker.

materials

vellum
baseball card holder sheet protector
cardstock
rub-ons
snap
photo corner
paper clip
safety pin
stickers
fiber
texture frames
clear embossing ink
adhesive
embossing powder
pearlescent powders
pen
chalk
ephemera

tools

heat tool with pen tip
embossing gun
scissors
paper trimmer
paint brush
sewing machine

materials

cardstock
papier-mâché portfolio
printed black rubber bands
black embossed paper
black ink
black buttons
black gesso
spray adhesive
gel medium
collected ephemera
art foil
elastics with metal tips (natural)
acetate transparencies
black duct tape
double-sided tape

tools

scissors
paper trimmer
craft knife
cutting mat
hole punch

ephemera portfolio

Linda Blinn

On this personalized portfolio, the artist has added ephemera on top of other ephemera in the form of Slash Pockets (see page 103). She mixes up the standard Slash Pocket by using transparencies and photocopied letters, and by making embellished double-slash pockets.

instructions

Affix black embossed paper to front and back of portfolio with spray adhesive. Paint top of portfolio and flap with black gesso.

For the large slash pocket, cut out a cardstock pocket the size of the portfolio adding a 1" (2.5 cm) border to the sides and bottom. Cover with color-copied ephemera and adhesive. Cut and fold in the 1" (2.5 cm) edges and glue to the portfolio. Cover portfolio sides and bottom with black duct tape. Collage ephemera and adhere with gel medium to the flap. Punch small holes and place the metal ends of elastics in each hole to hold more ephemera. Add black elastic to keep the top closed. Cut a black, printed elastic and place the ends through the holes in the top of the portfolio. Affix the ends with duct tape under the flap.

For the acetate transparency slash pockets, copy image of ephemera on to transparency film. Fashion the pocket by folding the transparency and cutting an angle on the top. Use black duct tape on the edges and place ephemera inside.

For the double slash pocket, fold a standard sized paper copy of ephemera in half. Cover all edges except the folded edge with double-stick tape. Apply foil to tape. With a craft knife, cut two curves in the top piece of paper. Highlight with black ink and black buttons. Put ephemera in each of the pockets created by the cuts. Add an acetate pocket at the bottom.

memories of lost and found book

Tim Holtz

A study in collected ephemera, this Dueling Accordion Pullout (see page 112) is like a museum of travel memorabilia, right down to the train tracks!

instructions

Create a front and back cover using the lid and the bottom of a wooden cigar box. Edge the cut sides of the cigar box covers using metal foil tape and antique. Cut strips of cardstock to create two basic accordions. Glue several strips together to achieve the length you want for your book. The accordion panels should be sized to fit the cigar box cover. Create a Dueling Accordion by interlocking them (see Dueling Accordion Pullout, page 112).

Use ink to age the edges of all the pages to create a worn vintage look. Stamp words with alphabet stamps on pages and collage each section to coordinate with the theme of the stamped word. Glue all objects with an adhesive that is nontoxic and dries clear. If you don't want to include the original paper items, scan or copy the image to use in your book. Affix ephemera and mica with glue or other attachments like eyelets, staples, brads, and clips.

Glue the covers to the ends of the Dueling Accordion Book and attach a measuring tape with a clasp for a closure to your book. Include other dimensional media to use to embellish your cover. Attach fibers to the tops of your book pages by threading through eyelets affixed in the centers of each page and secured to the covers.

materials

cigar box
cardstock
fibers
mica
embellishments
collected ephemera
ink
glue
metal foil tape
eyelets
staples
brads
clips
measuring tape
clasp

tools

bone folder
stamps
scissors
paper trimmer

materials

cardstock
patterned paper
eyelets
mini brads
label holders
office tag
charms
tags
tulle
metal embellishments
upholstery trims
staples
thread
adhesive
photograph

tools

sewing machine
scissors
paper trimmer
bone folder

instructions

Adhere patterned paper to card-stock to make a cover. Add a matted and tulle embellished feature photo with trim, mini brads, and titled label holder. Create a tag pouch pullout by tracing an office tag five times wide. Cut this out, score each section and accordion fold. Sew a small rectangle of tulle around three sides on each panel of the tag pouch pullout. Add decorative trim along the top of the tulle pouches by stitching only at the score lines. Attach the pullout to the page. Finish the pullout by copying and reducing photos and memorabilia, mounting them on cardstock and then embellishing them with eyelets, charms, tabs, staples, or an embellishment of choice. Tuck these into the pouches to aid in telling more of the story behind the photo.

memory scrapbook page

Sharon Soneff

Each panel of the Tag Pouch Pullout (see page 118) on this scrapbook page is filled with captivating photos and ephemera.

definitions collage (standing)

Carol Wingert

On this canvas memory collage, the artist imaginatively uses Laminated Tag Pullouts (see page 115) to highlight some "defining" journaling.

materials

decorative paper
nail heads
mini brads
stickers
embroidery thread
cardstock
aluminum tag
stretched canvas
charm
hat pin
paper napkin
adhesive
luggage tags
ink
paint
photograph

tools

foam stamps
scissors
paper trimmer
paint brush
sewing machine
computer and printer

instructions

Measure and cut four layers of paper (including paper napkin) to fit a 12" × 12" (30.5 × 30.5 cm) canvas. Add photos. Turn back two paper corners and secure with nail heads. Computer generate part of journal blocks and then add sticker letters. Cut and fit into two luggage tags. Trim tags and machine sew around the edges. Wrap embroidery thread around a strip of cardstock. Attach to a long metal tag with glue. Attach to layout with mini brads to form a strip to hold the luggage tag. Cut two strips of paper and layout to form an x. Glue down one side and attach the other side with decorative nail heads. Add hat pin and charm to the x. Insert second journaling tag. Paint and stamp canvas sides and glue layout onto the canvas.

materials

shipping envelopes
stenciled cardboard
ephemera
ledger paper
photographs
transparencies
vellum
art poster
spiral binding
twine and string
collage elements
wax
acrylic paints
matte medium

tools

spiral-coil binding machine
paint brush

envelope journal (below, standing)

Lynne Perrella

The artist used the Rolled-Up Hiding Place (see page 128) to affix some soft tendrils of painted twine onto her highly decorated art journal made of sturdy shipping envelopes.

instructions

The page surface is an old sheet of ledger paper, with various collage elements applied, including photos, scraps of stenciled cardboard, and ephemera. Monoprinting was added, as well as splatters of acrylic paints, and the finished page was coated with wax to create a silky smooth surface. Mixed in with the shipping envelopes are other papers of all kinds, including transparencies, vellum sheets, and even an art poster rescued from a scrap heap and trimmed down to fit into the book. The completed pages were punched with a coil binding machine, and the spiral binding was added.

materials

brass bee charm
honeycomb image
mini brads
acetate
spiral journal
paints
copper tape

tools

brushes
craft knife
alphabet stamp

bee journal (above, center)

Michelle Ward

The artist has employed the Window Box Hiding Place (see page 125) for an architecturally inspired journal cover.

instructions

A painted cover of a spiral journal is cut with a craft knife to create an opening. A window is formed by overlaying printed acetate, trimmed in copper tape, and then adhered with black mini brads. Beneath the window on the first page of the journal is a hidden brass bee charm.

precious little girls

Shannon Jones

This chocolatey scrapbook page safely stores a sugar and spice–filled book of little girls with a Lock and Key Hiding Place (see page 122).

instructions

Create a shadow box (see page 15). Trim cardstock to fit over top the foam board. Use acrylic paint and letter and architectural stamps to create the cover journaling and embellishments. Use paper flowers, brads, and acrylic paints to create the side border, dabbing paint on the flowers and brads to match the theme of the rest of the page.

Under the shadow box, layer brown cardstock and pink burlap. Lay the mini album down in the shadow box and mark two holes on either side of the book for eyelets (to lace the ribbon). Add pink eyelets and adhere the whole page together.

Insert brown ribbon from the top through the right side eyelet around the back of the layout and up through the left eyelet. Insert mini themed album and tie the ribbon, lock and key into place with knots.

Buy or create your own mini album. Use acrylic paints to create the flowers and to paint the outsides of the book. Use floss to sew buttons at the center of each flower. Use brown chalk on the entire cover and backside of the book. Scrapbook the inside of the album with your favorite pictures from an event or photo shoot.

materials

mini book
paper flowers
brads
patterned paper
foam core
photographs
ribbon
floss
buttons
lock and key
burlap
cardstock
eyelets
acrylic paint
adhesive
chalks

tools

foam stamps
stamps
punches
scissors
paper trimmer
paint brush

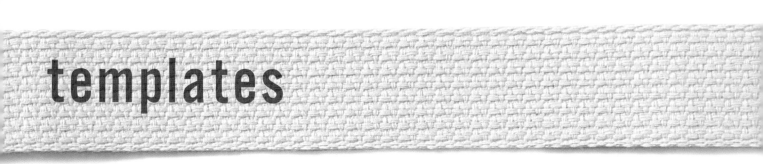

templates

All templates provided are sized for the projects in which they are used. They can be enlarged or reduced to suit a project of any size.

Vellum Pocket, Cowgirl Memory Book, page 28

Library Pocket, Lucy Locket, pages 24–25

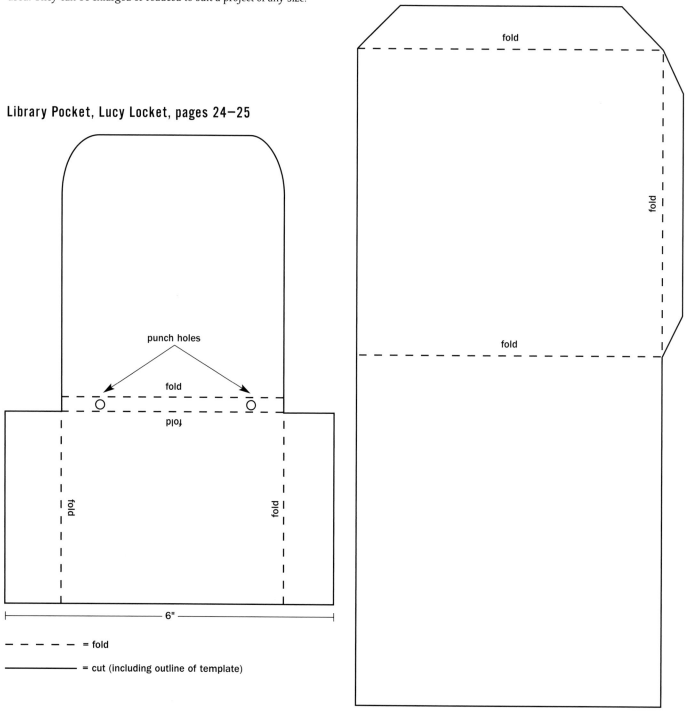

punch holes

fold

fold

fold

fold

⊢——— 6" ———⊣

– – – – = fold

——— = cut (including outline of template)

fold

– – – – = fold

Reinforcement Hiding Place, page 47

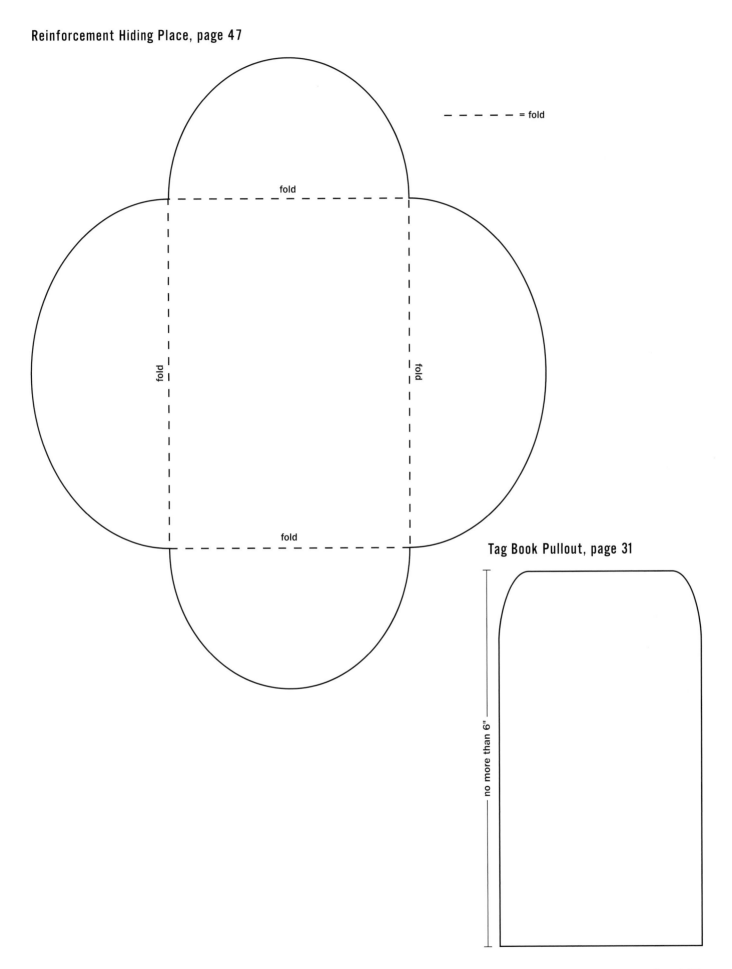

- - - - - = fold

fold

fold

fold

fold

Tag Book Pullout, page 31

no more than 6"

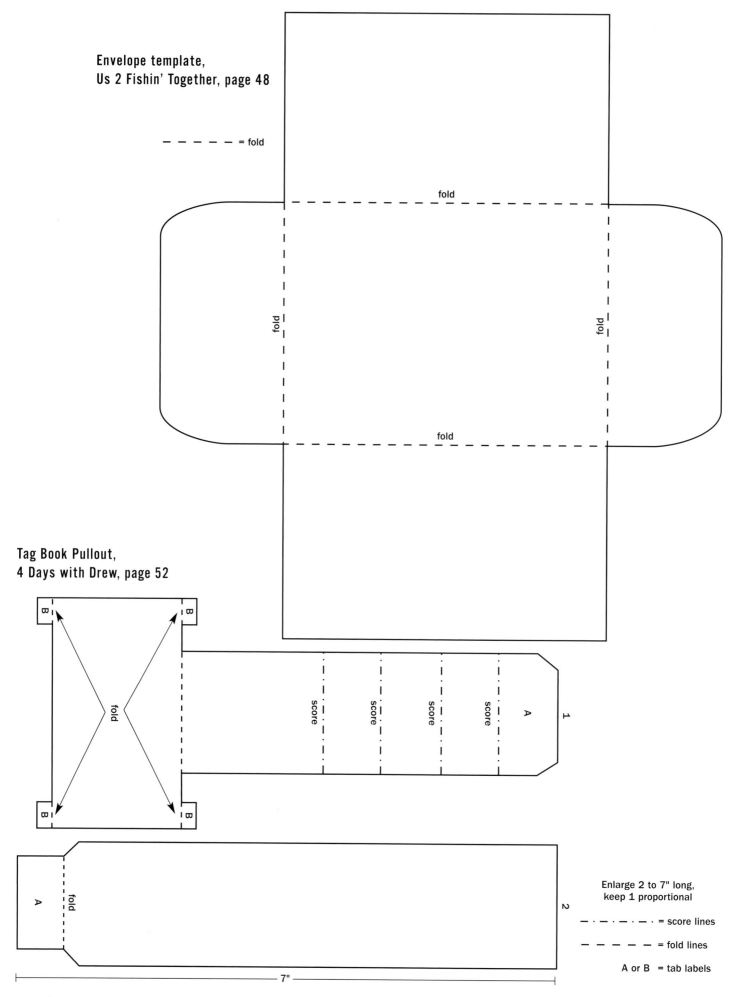

Envelope template,
Us 2 Fishin' Together, page 48

— — — — — = fold

fold

fold

fold

fold

Tag Book Pullout,
4 Days with Drew, page 52

B B

fold

B B

score

score

score

score

A

1

A

fold

2

Enlarge 2 to 7" long,
keep 1 proportional

— · — · — · — = score lines

— — — — — = fold lines

A or B = tab labels

7"

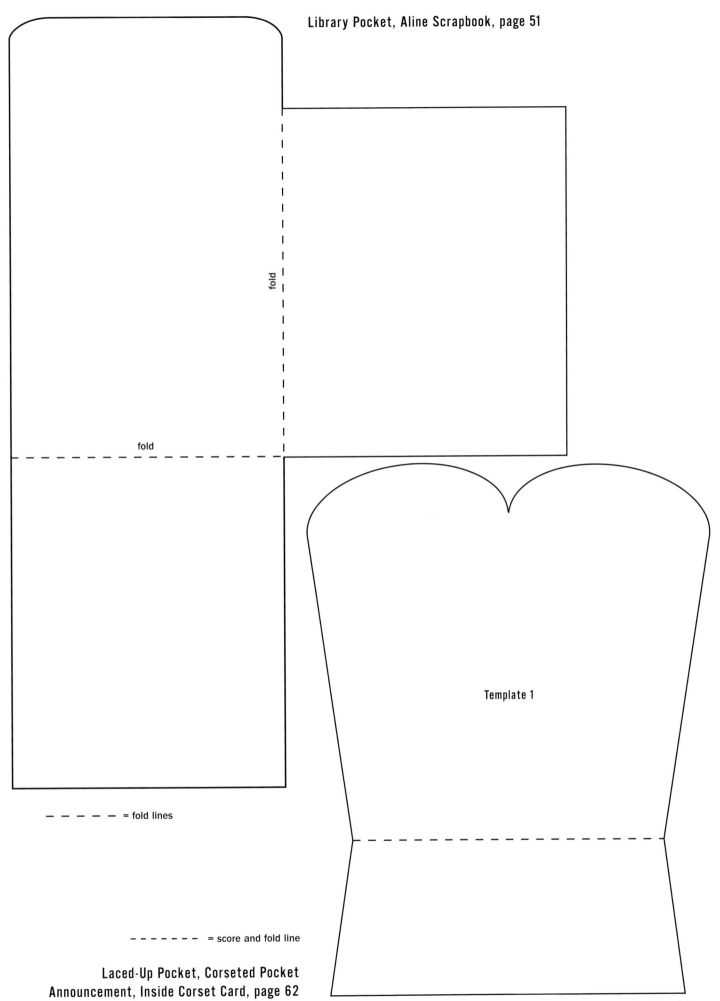

fold

fold

- - - - - = fold lines

- - - - - = score and fold line

Template 1

**Laced-Up Pocket, Corseted Pocket
Announcement, Inside Corset Card, page 62**

Laced-Up Pocket, Corseted Pocket Announcement,
Card Enclosure, page 62

Laced-Up Pocket,
Corseted Pocket
Announcement,
Corset Skirt, page 62

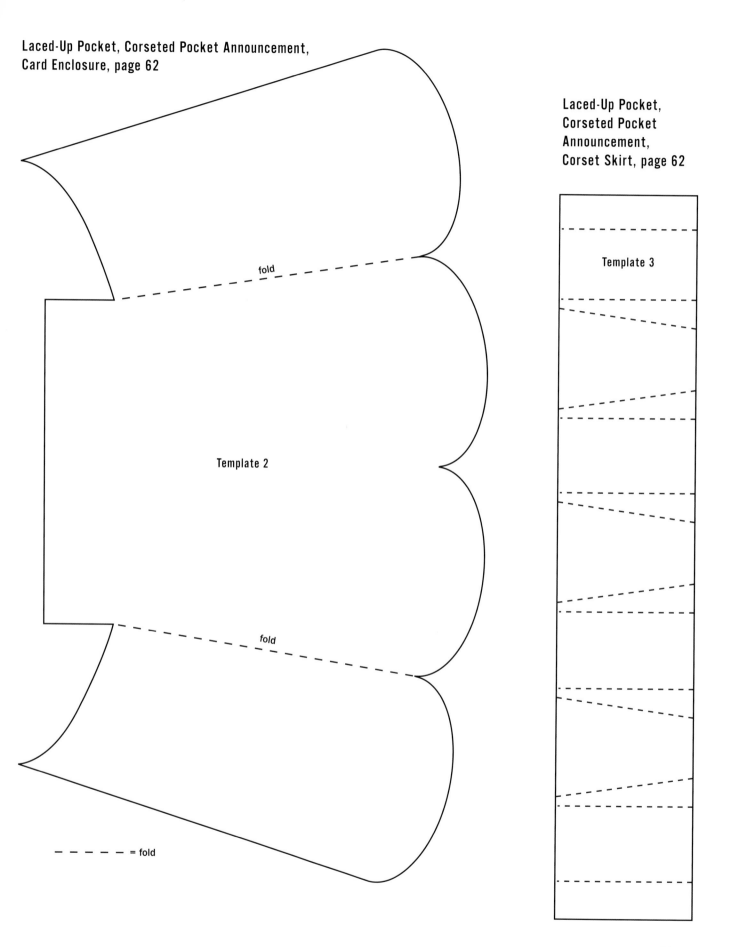

fold

fold

Template 2

Template 3

— — — — = fold

— — — — = score and fold lines

Slash Pocket, Discover Time, page 104

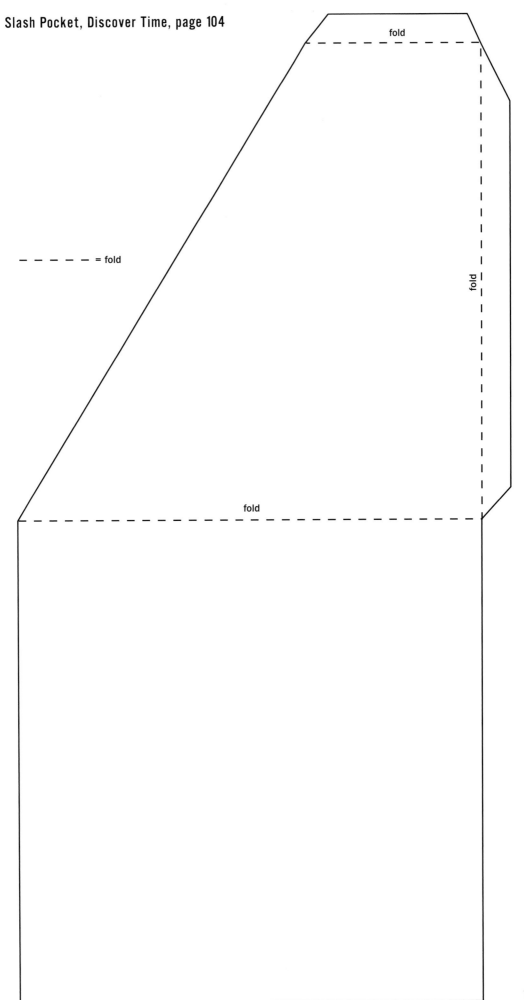

– – – – = fold

fold

fold

fold

contributors

Christine Adolph

Mixed-media floral collage, surface pattern design, and illustration are all ways to describe what keeps Christine busy. She has been a designer for ten years and enjoys working with foil imaging, collage, painting, and drawing with acrylics and watercolor. Christine has a BFA from Otis College of Art and Design and a MFA from Rhode Island School of Design. She has worked as a textile designer and is currently working as a part-time freelance designer focusing on licensing her artwork for the gift, home décor, and craft market. Christine has been published in *Legacy*, *Somerset Studio*, and *Inspirations* magazines as well as the books *Signatures*, *Material Visions*, and *Collage Cards*. She also has a line of floral and holiday stamps from Stampington and Company and a line of scrapbook paper and stickers from Creative Imaginations. Christine lives just steps from the ocean in beautiful San Clemente, California, with her husband and two little girls.

info@christineadolph.com
www.christineadolph.com

Jenna Beegle

Jenna Beegle used to spend her time creating with needle and thread before discovering the joys of paper crafting. Starting with scrapbooking, her paper crafting career became more varied and interesting than she could have expected. Though she says her college design teacher would faint to hear it, Jenna now works for Anna Griffin, Inc., creating lovely things, in addition to teaching stamping, scrapbooking, and altered techniques. Jenna's work has been seen in *Memory Makers*, *Legacy*, *Somerset Studio*, and *Paper Crafts* magazines.

Jennifer Francis Bitto

Jennifer has been interested in art her whole life but has been focused for the last five years on a clean, simple, straightforward approach to paper arts. She loves mixing metal findings and fabric with her paper art, and has been published in *Stamper's Sampler*, *Somerset Studio*, and *Legacy* magazines. She is currently teaching classes and working on a journal collaborative. Jennifer lives in Southern California.

takeflight4art@yahoo.com

Linda Blinn

Having confessed to being the biggest paper geek ever born, Linda Blinn is a writer, mixed-media artist, and class instructor. She is the former editor of "Mélange," a section of *Somerset Studio* magazine, and Special Projects Editor for art journal publications including the *Art Journal Calendar*, *True Colors*, and *Signatures*. Her art has appeared in *Victoria* magazine and *Artists' Journals and Sketchbooks* by Lynne Perrella.

She is continually amazed at the crossover in fabric, paper, jewelry, and collage and marvels at the endless possibilities it offers mixed-media artists—from scrapbooking all the way to fine art. Her biggest satisfaction comes from interviewing artists and capturing their message to inspire others. Teaching provides her with an opportunity to celebrate how students transform an idea and make it into something completely their own.

Linda lives with her husband, Tom, by the ocean in San Clemente, California, where she often has difficulty discerning between what is work and what is play. Her favorite quote is: "Personality is more important than beauty, but imagination is more important than both of them," by Laurette Taylor, an actress.

228 West Avenida Valencia
San Clemente, CA 92672 USA
ljblinn@pacbell.net.

Michelle Bodensteiner

Michelle has been an artist as long as she can remember. Her work is clean and crisp with soft coordinated colors and gentle contrasts that lean toward a classical style. She loves to experiment with color and layering and watching a piece unfold and grow to completion. She has been published in the *Rubber Stamper*, the *Stamper's Sampler*, *Rubberstampmadness*, and Stampington's *Inspirations*, as well as being the featured Guest Artist in 2002 for *Stamper's Sampler*. She has been a visiting artist on call for Stampington and Company and has been a participating artist in two art exhibits at the Loveland Museum Gallery. Michelle lives in Loveland, Colorado, the Gateway to Rocky Mountain National Park.

Jenni Bowlin

Jenni Bowlin resides in Nashville, Tennessee, with her husband and two young sons. She is a published designer and is a *Creating Keepsakes* 2003 Hall of Fame winner. Jenni is also an accomplished teacher, offering classes on a regular basis at Scrap It! in Hermitage, Tennessee, and teaches at stores and conventions across the country, including Creating Keepsakes University. She is the Creative Director for Li'l Davis Designs and is the designer of some of the company's newest product lines. You won't see many layouts from Jenni without tags, paint, or stamps, and she has a fondness for collage.

Li'l Davis Designs
17835 Sky Park Circle
Irvine, CA 92614 USA
949.838.0344
jenni@lildavisdesigns.com
www.lildavisdesigns.com

Katherine Brooks

Katherine started scrapbooking in 1997 shortly after the birth of her first child. She loved documenting her daughter's growth but along the way found a creative outlet in scrapbooking. Some of Katherine's favorite scrapbooking materials include polymer clay, patterned papers, and acrylic paints. In 2003 she became a full-time designer and instructor for Deluxe Designs. Katherine's first idea book, *Tagging Along*, was released in 2003, followed by *Card Crazy* and her own line of stickers and papers. Her book *Deluxe Techniques* was released in 2004. Katherine has been published numerous times in *Creating Keepsakes*, *Legacy*, and *Memory Makers* magazines. She is a *Creating Keepsakes* Hall of Famer and a *Memory Makers* Master. Katherine lives in Arizona with her husband of ten years and her two children, Meghan and Matt.

Karen Burniston

Karen is an independent designer and instructor from Littleton, Colorado, where she lives with her husband John and her twins, Karl and Emma. Karen hung up her hardhat after ten years in the road construction industry and put her engineering background to good use in the scrapbook industry, both in her layout design and her product design. Karen travels to numerous conventions and universities to teach on behalf of Creative Imaginations, which licenses her Scrapperware line of products.

Karen started stamping in 1991 after walking into a rubber stamp store, and has been published frequently in *Rubberstampmadness*. After her children were born, she became interested in scrapbooking and was published in *Creating Keepsakes, Memory Makers, Paper Crafts,* and *Scrapbooks Etc.* magazines, and was named a winner in the *Creating Keepsakes* 2002 Hall of Fame contest. She has contributed to several scrapbooking idea books including *Hot Looks for Scrapbooks* by *Creating Keepsakes*.

info@scrapperware.com
www.scrapperware.com

Beth Cote

Beth Cote is a professional mixed media artist and nationally recognized altered book artist. She has taught art to both children and adults for over ten years. Cote's lifelong passion for both art and the written word has led her to national recognition as the foremost artist of altered books—an artistic expression that combines elements of rubberstamping, collage, and scrapbooking to transform a book into a work of art.

311 South Elida
Winnebago, IL 61088 USA
www.alteredbook.com

Cheryl Darrow

Cheryl has been involved in the art field for twenty years and travels around the country teaching various classes, including calligraphy, bookbinding, paper making, paste papers, card construction, metal effects, fabric necklaces, doll making, PMC jewelry, altered books, and journals. She is the author of two books, *Die Art One* and *Die Art Two*, both of which cover creative uses for die cuts. She has designed die cuts and rubber stamps for major manufacturers. She loves finding ways to incorporate calligraphy in her art, and her latest passion is working in metal.

www.tensecondsstudio.com

Dana DiCicco

Dana, who has a BFA in painting and drawing, uses a mixed media, vintage style mixed with a contemporary and humorous twist in her work. She is the cofounder and sole artist of River City Rubber Works as well as Waxing Nostalgia. She has been published in *Rubber Stamper, Rubberstampmadness*, and *Rubber Stampin' Retailer*, and has authored a series of books by River City Rubber Works as well as *Heritage Photo Journals* by Pinecone Press. She is currently working on developing Waxing Nostalgia. When she's not busy at work, you can find Dana living in Wichita, Kansas, in a big red barn!

River City Rubber Works & Waxing Nostalgia
5555 South Meridian
Wichita, KS 67217-3721 USA
316.529.8656
877.735.2276 (toll-free)
info@rivercityrubberworks.com
info@waxingnostalgia.com
www.waxingnostalgia.com

Holly Sar Dye

A weekend book artist and paper crafter, Holly Sar Dye dwells in Granada Hills, California, with her husband of twenty years, Philip, and their son, Alec. She incorporates origami and rubber stamping techniques in her art. Holly is a teacher for Simi Valley Unified School District and UCLA Education Extension. Additionally, she teaches weekend and evening art classes in the Los Angeles area. She shares her love for making books with her students, and in turn teaches them the art and craft of book artistry. Her work has been featured in *Time* magazine.

bookartist@bufobufo.com

Suzi Finer

Suzi has never had any classical training, but she's been an artist her whole life. When she's working she tries not to think about it and "just does it." She loves working with acrylics and painting on wood panels and foam core. She loves murals, but won't climb a ladder; loves sculpting, but doesn't like to get her hands dirty. Suzi doesn't limit herself to any one style or any one chosen media. She is even a "master" cake decorator and has had her cakes published in *People* and other magazines. Suzi is very busy running her shop, Suzi Finer, Artworks and Artware, and doing side projects when they come up. She is also creating a line of decorative papers and rubber stamps. Suzi and her store are located in Beverly Hills, California.

417 North Canon Drive
Beverly Hills, CA 90210 USA
310.360.1800
suzi@suzifiner.com
www.suzifiner.com

Claudine Hellmuth

Claudine is a nationally known collage and mixed-media artist. Her work has been chosen as fine art poster designs, featured in numerous magazines, used as book cover artwork, published as rubber stamps, drink coasters, and more. Many of Claudine's products can be found nationally in stores such as Target, JoAnn's, and the Bombay Co.

Claudine teaches mixed-media collage workshops in the United States and Canada, and wrote a book about her techniques titled *Collage Discovery Workshop,* published by North Light Books. In 2004 she was a guest on the *Carol Duvall Show* on HGTV and demonstrated techniques from her book.

With a BFA in fine art from the Corcoran College of Art, Claudine approaches collage the old-fashioned way. She enjoys the challenge of working with a variety of materials and cutting, pasting, and painting her artworks by hand. Her studio and home are in Orlando, Florida, where she lives with her husband, Paul, and their very spoiled four-legged children—Toby the wonder dog, and Melvis and Maggie, the cats. Please visit Claudines's website, www.collageartist.com, to learn more about her.

Tim Holtz

Stamp artist Tim Holtz is the designer and senior educator for Ranger Industries, one of the leading manufacturers of innovative inks and embossing and craft products. His techniques are creative and inspiring for stampers of all levels. Tim travels extensively to national trade shows and stores across the country to educate and introduce people to his world of inks, papers, and much more. Tim has been a frequent guest on HGTV's *The Carol Duvall Show*, and his projects can been seen regularly in stamping and scrapbooking magazines. Tim also has his own signature product lines with Ranger and his own DVD titled *An Altered Journey* with Tim Holtz by PageSage.

His mantra is, "Creativity is an endless journey where we should always take the scenic route."

www.timholtz.com

Shannon Jones

Shannon has been a professional scrapbooker since 2002 and was a *Creating Keepsakes* 2002 Hall of Fame winner. She is the author of *Scrapbooking with Style* and is a member of the *Creating Keepsakes* Creative Editorial team. She enjoys using stitched accents in her feminine-style pages and is regularly published in *Creating Keepsakes* magazines and books. She is currently busy teaching at *Creating Keepsakes* conventions and universities. When she's not traveling, Shannon is at home in Mesa, Arizona, with her three daughters and her husband of fourteen years, David.

Stephanie McAtee

Stephanie lives in Kansas City, Missouri, and has been scrapbooking since 2000. She's always had a passion for journaling and photography, and enjoys using dimensional, interactive elements in her art. She hopes to draw people into her work to embrace the whole piece—and get it. Her hope is that one day her boys, Bobby and Ethan, will get her books and know what she was thinking and feeling, and understand the depth that she put into her art. The boys are her subjects that she's "crazy in love with."

stephlynnmcatee@aol.com

Rebecca Odom

Rebecca likes to mix classic clean lines with a shabby chic style. She has been a graphic designer for six years and a scrapbook designer for the past two. She loves typography and aging paper. Rebecca is the designer of the award-winning *Phrase Café*, as well as *Color Oasis*, *Tag Types*, and *Stickersaurus*. She has been published in *EK Success* and *Scrapbook Borders* publications. She is currently working on class projects and other product samples. Rebecca lives in Rio Rancho, New Mexico.

Writer's Block Publishing, Inc.
1380 Rio Rancho Boulevard, #224
Rio Rancho, NM 87124 USA
becky@writersblockpublishing.com

Lynne Perrella

Lynne is a mixed-media artist, author, designer, and workshop instructor. Her interests include collage, assemblage, one-of-a-kind books, and art journals. Her first book, *Artists' Journals and Sketchbooks* was published by Rockport Publishers' Quarry Books imprint. She frequently contributes stories and artwork to various paper arts publications, and serves on the advisory board of two magazines, *Somerset Studio* and *Legacy*. She teaches art workshops throughout the United States and abroad, and exhibits fine art collage in galleries throughout the Berkshire Mountains.

P. O. Box 194
Ancram, NY 12502 USA
www.LKPerrella.com

Marta Simmons-Wiechmann

Marta Simmons-Wiechmann has spent the last twenty-six years in marketing, advertising, design, and print production, including a focus on greeting cards and custom wedding invitations for the last three years.

She has always loved paper and is forever creating something with it. She has a contemporary style that often leans towards whimsical and is very sensitive to texture. Her favorite tool has long been her X-Acto knife and she has often referred to herself as a "knife artist" (although she did discover a wonderful pair of scissors a couple of years ago, of which she grows increasingly fond with each use).

Marta is actively involved in the study and promotion of calligraphy and the book arts. She has received several awards during her career for design and print. The wedding invitation she produced five years ago for her own wedding received a merit award from an international design competition for *HOW Magazine* and was showcased in the *2000 HOW Magazine Design Annual*.

Marta lives in Denton, Texas, and is currently working on a line of wedding invitations to be introduced at a national bridal show in Dallas.

940.382.4090
martalynn@charter.net
www.belletristdesignloft.com

Rhonda Solomon

Rhonda is funky, or at least that's what her work exudes. Her way of using different elements in unexpected ways is part of her signature style. She has been an artist since she could hold a crayon and regularly uses paint and inks in her work. Rhonda has been published in many scrapbooking publications and enjoys teaching and creating new product lines. She is currently working on creating classes for *Creating Keepsakes* University and on developing her new product lines. Scrapbooking is her hobby and she loves to see the bonds it creates and friendships that form among the artists. When Rhonda isn't busy sharing her ideas with others while traveling, she lives in Snowflake, Arizona.

Sharon Soneff

Sharon Soneff has been transferring her memories to the crafted page for nearly two decades. Pairing Sharon's love for lettering, watercolor, and design with her beloved hobby of scrapbooking seemed like a natural progression. But in so doing she birthed a new business, Sonnets, in which she brings to life the papers, stickers, and embellishments of her dreams.

When not creating new artwork for Sonnets, Sharon keeps busy as a wife and mother at her coastal Southern California home.

Sonnets
P.O. Box 4243
San Clemente, CA 92674 USA
949.369.0281
www.sonnetsbysharon.com

Jeannine Stein

Jeannine's style borders on the eclectic, and she has been working in the paper and book arts for about eight years. She enjoys working with metal and incorporating books and book binding into projects. She currently teaches and designs for Suzi Finer, Artworks and Artware of Beverly Hills, California, and enjoys working on altered books and learning new book binding techniques.

jsteinelson@yahoo.com

Allison Strine

Allison Strine is a mixed media artist who lives in Atlanta, Georgia. She loves working with many mediums, including paper, paints, fabrics, and polymer clay. Her work has been published in national scrapbook magazines.

allisonstrine@mindspring.com

Darcee Thompson

Darcee has always loved art and has been a scrapbooker since 1998. She loves to add texture to her work with techniques like embossing, stitching, or transferring texture. Darcee has been published in *Creating Keepsakes* magazine and *Scrapbooking with Style,* and is a *Creating Keepsakes* 2002 Hall of Fame winner. Darcee lives in Preston, Idaho.

Michelle Ward

Michelle is a designer living in Piscataway, New Jersey, with her husband and their three young children. She has been a rubber stamp designer for ten years and recently started a company, Green Pepper Press. Michelle primarily works with paper and paint in art journals, altered books, and on canvas. Some of her work has been published in the magazine *Somerset Studio,* as well as the books *Artists' Journals and Sketchbooks* by Lynne Perrella, *Altered Books, Collaborative Journals, and Other Adventures in Bookmaking* by Holly Harrison, *Stamp Artistry* by Ricë Freeman-Zachery and *True Colors* by Stampington and Company.

Green Pepper Press
P. O. Box 73
Piscataway, NJ 08855 USA
grnpep@optonline.net
www.greenpepperpress.com

Carol Wingert

Carol teaches paper and book arts workshops at Memory Lane near her home in Gilbert, Arizona. She has taught nationally at CKU, and internationally at the Inspirational Scrapbook Convention in Australia. Carol has been published regularly in *Legacy* magazine and *Creating Keepsakes* magazine, and won *Creating Keepsakes* Hall of Fame Honorable Mention awards in 2002 and 2003. She was a contributing artist to Autumn Leaves' *Designing with Photos, Designing with Words,* and *7 Gypsies in Paris,* and was lead artist in *The Book Book.* Carol has also contributed to several books for Design Originals, including *Altered Style Scrapbooks.* She lives with her husband (and best friend), Vern, and their daughter, Ashley.

745 North Gilbert Rd, #124
PMB 186
Gilbert, AZ 85234 USA
carolwingertaz@msn.com

supply contributors

Special thanks to the following manufacturers for contributing their products for use in this book.

K and Company
8500 Northwest River Park Drive
Pillar #136
Parkville, MO 64152 USA
Tel: 816.389.4150
Toll free: 888.244.2083
www.kandcompany.com

Making Memories
1168 West 500 North
Centerville, UT 84014 USA
www.makingmemories.com
Products for scrapbookers, artists, crafters,
and card makers

Quickutz
1365 West 1250 South
Orem, UT 84058 USA
Tel: 801.765.1144
Toll free: 888.702.1146
www.quickutz.com
Portable, accessible die-cutting

ReadySet Tools
705 North 1000 West Suite 11
Centerville, UT 84014 USA
Tel: 801.292.6164
RSSales@readysettools.com
www.readysettools.com
Eyelets and snaps

Scrapworks
3038 Specialty Circle, Suite C
Salt Lake City, UT 84115 USA
hello@scrapworks.com
www.scrapworks.com

Tsukineko
17640 Northeast 65th Street
Redmond, WA 98052 USA
Tel: 425.883.7733
sales@tsukineko.com
www.tsukineko.com

The Vintage Workshop
P.O. Box 30237
Kansas City, MO 64112 USA
Tel: 913.648.2700
www.thevintageworkshop.com
Printable inkjet media as well as artwork and
project inspirations, inkjet fabrics, papers,
and crafting products

Added thanks to the following three companies who went beyond the call of duty and supplied the contributing artists with their products as well.

3M
Tel: 888.3M HELPS (364.3577)
www.3m.com

Prism
P. O. Box 25068
Salt Lake City UT 84125 USA
Tel: 866.901.1002
customerservice@prismpapers.com
www.prismpaper.com
Wide selection of scrapbooking paper

Walnut Hollow Farm, Inc.
1409 State Road 23
Dodgeville, WI 53533 USA
Tel: 800.950.5101
www.walnuthollow.com
High quality, innovative, unfinished wood
products, clockmaking supplies, woodburning
and woodcarving tools, and instructional
books with patterns and techniques for the
beginner as well as the advanced artist

I encourage you to look into these companies and their wonderful products!

product manufacturers by project

Each project in this book is listed here by page number to help you locate manufacturers for the supplies used. To locate more information about a specific manufacturer see Resources, page 155.

Page 21, Page Pocket
Cardstock (Prism), adhesive (3M), circle punch, scissors, and paper trimmer.

Page 22, Diary of a Secret Princess Altered Book
Cardstock (Prism), decorative paper (K & Co., Anna Griffin), tissue paper, handmade paper, glassine envelope (Silver Crow Creations), printed acetate (K & Co), ribbon, paper flowers (Making Memories), old children's book, flower eyelets, alphabet charms (Making Memories), glitter (Magic Scraps), trim, soft gel gloss (Golden), fluid acrylics (Golden), industrial strength tape, adhesive (3M), inks (Stampin' Up!, Ranger), sponge dauber, circle punch, craft knife, scissors, paper trimmer.

Page 24, Library Pocket
Cardstock (Prism), adhesive (3M), bone folder, scissors, paper trimmer, and template (see page 138).

Page 25, Lucy Locket's Pocket Purse
Cardstock (Prism), decorative paper (Anna Griffin), vellum paper, beaded trim, brads (Making Memories), flower nail head (Jewelcraft), eyelets, ribbon, double-stick tape (3M), ink (Tsukineko), sponge dauber, bone folder, craft knife, scissors, eyelet setting tools (Readyset), paper trimmer, template (see page 138).

Page 26, Vellum Pocket
Vellum, vellum adhesive (3M), scoring tool, circle punch, decorative-edged scissors (Fiskars), scissors, ruler.

Page 28, Cowgirl Memory Book
Template (see page 143), vellum, cardstock (Prism), handmade paper, colored key tag (Making Memories), small tag, journaled text, mat board, page pebbles (Making Memories), paper flower, elastic cord, metal word plates (K & Co), nail heads (Jewelcraft), adhesive (3M), vellum adhesive (3M), ink (Stampin Up!), colored pencils (Berol), bone folder, scissors, paper cutter.

Page 31, Tag Book Pullout
Tags (pre-made, punched, die cut, or traced from supplied template, page 139), cardstock (Prism), attachments (brad, eyelets, snaps, or staples), hole punch or craft knife, scissors.

Page 32, Tokens of Friendship Pullout Mini Book
Shrink plastic (inkjet printable for computer users), cardstock (Prism), decorative paper (Making Memories, Anna Griffin), cardboard letter stencil, slide holder (DMD), message bottle (7 Gypsies), typewriter key frame (7 Gypsies), eyelets, metal spine (7 Gypsies), fibers, bath salts, ribbon charms (Making Memories), printed ribbon, children's illustration, stickers (Making Memories), adhesive (3M), double stick removable tape (3M), foam tape squares (3M), dimensional glaze, ink (Stampin' Up!), staples (Making Memories), embossing powder, chalks (Craf-T), punches (heart, circle, shoe), stamps (Just For Fun), decorative scissors (Fiskars), hole punch, eyelet setter (Readyset), craft knife, cutting mat, stapler, scissors, paper cutter, computer or alphabet stamps (for journaling).

Page 34, Flap Pullout
Cardstock (Prism), eyelets, hole punch, eyelet setter (Readyset), scissors, and paper trimmer.

Page 35, Sunflower Fields Altered Book
Decorative paper (Anna Griffin, K & Co), ribbon, stickers (K & Co), rub-ons (Making Memories), paper flowers (Making Memories), ribbon charms (Making Memories), charm plaques (Making Memories), bow (Anna Griffin), black pen, craft knife, scissors.

Page 37, Accordion Pullout
Cardstock (Prism), mat board, metal frames (Scrapworks), scissors, paper trimmer, bone folder.

Page 38, Melanie's Smile Memory Art Book
Cardstock (Prism), handmade paper, water color paper, foam core, clear frame stickers (K & Co), paper flowers (Making Memories), brads (Making Memories), ribbon, ink (Stampin' Up!), water color paint and brush, removable double-stick tape (3M), industrial strength double-stick tape, stamp (PSX), alphabet stamp (Making Memories), scissors, paper trimmer, craft knife, sewing machine.

Page 41, Sealed Envelope Hiding Place
Cardstock (Prism), envelopes, wax seals (Creative Imaginations), stickers (K & Co), photo corners, pen.

Page 42, Hunter Cooks Scrapbook Page
Cardstock (Prism), decorative paper (K & Co, Anna Griffin), ribbon, printed twill tape, sticker seals (Creative Imaginations), metal embellishments (7 Gypsies), conchos (Scrapworks), rub-ons (Making Memories), staples (Making Memories), ceramic tag, metal plaque (Making Memories), ink (Stampin' Up!), adhesive (3M), plastic envelope template system (Provocraft), die cut alphabet (Quickutz), sewing machine, sanding block or sand paper, scissors, paper trimmer.

Page 44, Matchbook Hiding Place
Cardstock (Prism), brads, jute, ink stamps (Stampin' Up!), pinking scissors (Fiskars), scissors, paper trimmer, stapler, hole punch, square punches.

Page 45, Babies and Stress Relief Bubbles Gift Cards

Cardstock (Prism), decorative paper (Crafts Etc., Anna Griffin, K & Co, The Vintage Workshop), ribbon, charm, concho (Scrapworks), brads (Making Memories), safety pins (Making Memories), ink (Stampin' Up!, Ranger), vintage clip-art (The Vintage Workshop), foam tape (3M), sanding block or sand paper, pinking scissors (Fiskars), scissors, paper trimmer, sponge daubers, sewing machine.

Page 47, Reinforcement Hiding Place

Cardstock (Prism), circle punch, brads, tie (twine, raffia, yarn, or other fiber), craft knife, scissors, and paper cutter.

Page 48, Us 2 Fishin' Together

Cardstock (Prism), decorative paper (K & Co), children's illustration, library due date slip, old playing card, label holder (Making Memories), photo turns (7 Gypsies), old map, canvas, stickers (EK Success), eyelet snaps (Cloud 9), brads, nails, mini label maker (Dymo), jute, translucent embossing paste (Dreamweaver Stencils), matte gel medium (Liquitex), acrylic paints (Liquitex), acrylic extender (Liquitex), graining tool (United Gilsonite Laboratories), brass templates, hammer, craft knife, scissors, paper cutter, template (see page 140).

Page 50, Words Give Our Hearts Wings Papier-Mâché Book Box by Michelle Bodensteiner

Cardstock (Prism), decorative paper (7 Gypsies, K & Co., Autumn Leaves, Two Hands Papierie, Creative Imaginations), papier-mâché box, antique postcard (Victorian Trading Company), ribbons (Making Memories), brads (Creative Impressions), frame (Making Memories), key (Making Memories), stamps (Hampton Arts, Hero Arts Limited Edition), postcard tile (Limited Edition), matchboxes (Limited Edition), paper roses, stickers (Victorian Trading Company), tissue paper, ink, acrylic paint, adhesive, sponge, scissors, paper cutter.

Page 51, Altered Book with Paper Bag Pocket by Beth Cote

Kraft paper bag, *The Ephemera Book or CD* by Beth Cote, decorative paper and vellum (Design Originals, Making Memories), slide mounts (Design Originals), rickrack, vintage file folder, tea stained tags (American Tag), craft cork, old button and vintage earring parts, chalk ink (ColorBox, adhesive (Thermo web, Uhu), stamps (Fred Mullet, Post Modern Design), scissors, paper trimmer.

Page 51, Aline Scrapbook Page by Jeannine Stein

Cardstock (Prism), decorative paper (Paper Adventures, K & Co., The Gifted Line), metal letters (Making Memories), paper flowers (Making Memories), photo turns (Making Memories), tassels (Judikins), acrylic paint (Making Memories), adhesive (3M), foam stamps (Making Memories), rubber stamps (Memory Box), scissors, paper trimmer.

Page 52, 4 Days of Drew Scrapbook Page by Karen Burniston

Cardstock (Prism), decorative papers (K & Co., Wordsworth, Creative Imaginations, Karen Foster, Carolee's Creations), folded tile (Creative Imaginations), rub-ons (Creative Imaginations), brads, wire charm (Westrim), photo corners (Canson), stickers (Creative Imaginations, Pebbles, Tumblebeasts), ink (Tsukineko, Ranger, Clearsnap), adhesive (3M), label maker (Dymo), pinking shears, paper crimper, rubber stamps (Making Memories, Purple Onion Designs, Above the Mark, Art Impressions, Lasting Impressions, PSX, Ma Vinci's Reliquary), template (see page 140), scissors, paper trimmer.

Page 53, Wedding Day 1924 by Dana DiCicco

Cardstock (Prism), decorative paper (Paper Parachute), vellum (Papers By Catherine), acetate (K & Co.), leather-like paper (K & Co.), brass hinges (National), eyelets (River City Rubber Works, American Tag), ink (River City Rubber Works, Ranger), double sided photo/document tape (3M), craft adhesive (3M), stamps (River City Rubber Works), scissors, paper trimmer.

Page 54, Triangular Accordion Book by Holly Sar Dye

Book board, cardstock (Prism), decorative paper (Paper Source, EK Success, K & Co., Creative Imaginations), transparent artistic sheets (Magic Scraps), ribbon, adhesive, craft knife (X-Acto), paper trimmer, bone folder, and quote book (*Breathing on Your Own* by Richard Kehl, *Book of Positive Quotations* by John Cook).

Page 55, What is Life? Collage by Cheryl Darrow

Small frames, decorative paper, ribbon, copper mesh (PostModern Rubber Stamps), brads, wire, cardstock, acrylic paint, decoupage glue, adhesive, walnut ink (PostModern Rubber Stamps), tape, rubber stamp (PostModern Rubber Stamps), glue brush, Japanese hole punch, dowel.

Page 56, "C"—Christian James Scrapbook Page by Jenni Bowlin

Cardstock (Prism), ribbon (Li'l Davis Designs), book plate (Li'l Davis Designs), bottle cap (Li'l Davis Designs), rub-ons (Li'l Davis Designs), epoxy numbers (Li'l Davis Designs), safety pins (Li'l Davis Designs), mini brads (Bazzill), woven label (Me and My Big Ideas), vintage ledger, waxed linen, jewelry tags, ink, blue paint, adhesive (3M, Glue Dots International), stamps (PostModern Design), scissors, paper trimmer.

Page 57, We Grow Collage by Allison Strine

Ribbon (Making Memories), flowers (Making Memories), transparencies (Creative Imaginations), sailcloth, felt, jeans, burlap, lace, earring, buttons, adhesive (3M), paint, sewing machine, scissors, paper trimmer.

Page 61, Laced-Up Pocket

Cardstock (Prism), adhesive (3M), laces (raffia, twine, jute, etc), bone folder, hole punch, scissors, and paper trimmer.

Page 62, Corseted Pocket Announcement

Cardstock (Prism), patterned paper (Anna Griffin), ribbon, letter stickers (Anna Griffin), thin fiber, paper flower, printed journal boxes (Anna Griffin), small buttons, needle, stamp (Paper Inspiration), hole punch, scissors (Fiskars), paper trimmer, templates (pages 141–142),

Page 64, Catch-All Pocket

Cardstock or vellum (Prism), waxed string (Scrapworks), brads (Making Memories), staples (Making Memories), or a sewing machine.

Page 65, Curls and Cocoa Petals
Cardstock (Prism), decorative paper (KI Memories, Making Memories), vellum, alphabet stickers (KI Memories), conchos (Scrapworks), waxed string (Scrapworks), ball chain and connector, letter clips (Scrapworks), markers (EK Success), foam tape squares (3M), bone folder or Popsicle stick, corner rounder, craft knife, cutting mat, scissors, paper trimmer.

Page 67, Accordion Pocket
Envelopes, glue (3M), scissors, and paper trimmer.

Page 68, Snow Fun Shadow Box Collage
Cardstock (Prism), decorative paper (EK Success, Making Memories), printed tissue paper (7 Gypsies), memory windows (3M), inkjet waterslide decals (Lazertran), stickers (Making Memories), metal alphabets (Colorbok), metal embellishments (Scrapworks), printed ribbon (Making Memories), staples (Making Memories), absorbent ground medium (Golden), soft gel gloss (Golden), waxed twine (Scrapworks), ink (Stampin' Up!), adhesive (3M), foam tape squares (3M), alphabet and date stamps (Making Memories), needle tool, plastic envelope template system (Colozzle), pinking scissors (Fiskars), sponge dauber, paint brush, bone folder, scissors, paper trimmer.

Page 71, Flip/Flop Pullout
Cardstock (Prism), mat board, adhesive (3M), removable double-sided tape (3M), bone folder, scissors, and paper trimmer.

Page 72, She Loves Daddy Memory Book
Cardstock (Prism), decorative paper (Anna Griffin, K & Co), stickers (K & Co), metal handle (Foofala), old book pages, printed rubber band (7 Gypsies), waxed twine (Scrapworks), decorative clips (Scrapworks), paper tags (Making Memories), metal photo corners (Making Memories), woven photo corners (Making Memories), brads (Making Memories), rub-ons (Making Memories), paper flowers (Making Memories), printed ribbon (Making Memories), staples (Making Memories), snap tape, foam tape squares (3M), ink (Stampin' Up!), acrylic paint, sponge dauber, circle and square punch, bone folder, sanding block or sand paper, scissors, paper trimmer.

Page 74, Swing Pullout
Cardstock (Prism), fasteners, reinforcements, extended eyelets, ball chain, ribbon, metal rings, hole punch, scissors, paper trimmer, eyelet tools (Readyset).

Page 75, This Place is a Circus Swing Photo Journal
Cardstock (Prism), decorative paper (Anna Griffin), mat board, children's book pages, ribbons, ball chain with closure, ribbon charm (Making Memories), metal plaques (Making Memories), paper tags (Making Memories), rub-ons (Making Memories), waxed twine (Scrapworks), decorative clips (Scrapworks), adhesive (3M), ink (Stampin' Up!), sponge dauber, sanding block or sand paper, craft knife, bone folder, hole punch, paper trimmer.

Page 77, Mini Book Pullout
Cardstock (Prism), waxed twine (Scrapworks), hole punches, binding tools, binding spines, needle tool.

Page 78, Home 2004 book
Cardstock (Prism), printed blueprint tissue paper (7 Gypsies), screw binding posts, black twine, hardware fastener assortment, label holder (Making Memories), alphabet and date stamps (Making Memories), ink (Ranger), scissors, hole punch, glue stick (3M), bone folder, needle tool, paper trimmer, eyelet setting tools (Readyset).

Page 81, Secret Enclosure Hiding Place
Cardstock (Prism), embellishments (7 Gypsies, Making Memories), ink (Stampin' Up!), scissors, paper trimmer, bone folder, craft knife, adhesive (3M).

Page 82, All Boy, All Ben Scrapbook Page
Cardstock (Prism), decorative paper (K & Co, Anna Griffin), printed acetate (K & Co), page tabs (Avery), rub-ons (Making Memories), square brads (Making Memories), cut down paint brush, needle and thread, leaves, foam core, fluid acrylics (Golden), soft gel gloss medium (Golden), adhesive (3M), black writing pen, die cut alphabets (Quickutz), paint brush, scissors, paper trimmer.

Page 84, Page Flap Hiding Place
Cardstock (Prism), gold locks (7 Gypsies), swimsuit strap (Prym-Dritz), brads (Making Memories), frog enclosure (Wrights), ink (Ranger), embossing powder, scissors, paper trimmer, craft knife.

Page 85, Pilot's Log
Cardstock (Prism), self-adhesive metal paper (Magic Scraps), metal quote stickers (Making Memories), stamps (Making Memories), metal photo corners (Making Memories), silver locks (7 Gypsies), suspender clips (Prym-Dritz), ribbon (Making Memories), ink (Stampin' Up!, Ranger), foam tape (3M), industrial-strength tape, scissors, paper trimmer, sewing machine, foam cushion, stickers (K & Co), rub-ons (Making Memories), craft knife, black writing pen.

Page 87, All-in-One Hiding Place
Cardstock (Prism), adhesive (3M), die cuts or large punches (Sizzix), bone folder, scissors, and paper trimmer.

Page 88, We're Living Out of Boxes Moving Announcement
Cardstock (Prism), jute, mica, glassine envelopes (Silver Crow Creations), tissue paper, alphabet stamps (Making Memories), inks (Stampin' Up!, Tsukineko), adhesive (3M), sponge dauber, scissors, paper trimmer.

Page 90, Poppets in Pockets Journal by Claudine Hellmuth
Journal (7 Gypsies), waxed linen (7 Gypsies), cardstock (Prism), button, markers (Sakura), acrylic paint (Golden), glue stick (3M), scissors, paper trimmer.

Page 90, Cigar Box Photo Shrine by Jenna Beegle
Cardstock (Prism), decorative paper (Design Originals), burlap, ribbon (DiBona Designs), pearls (Blue Moon Beads), label holder (Li'l Davis Designs), sea shells, cigar box, transparency (3M), paint (Jaquard), gel medium (Golden), fluid acrylics (Golden), ink (Memories), adhesive (3M), stamps (Hero Arts), heat tool (Walnut Hollow), scissors, paper trimmer.

Page 91, Sunshine State Scrapbook Page by Katherine Brooks
Stickers (Deluxe Designs), patterned paper (Carolee's Creations), cardstock (Prism), vellum (Bazzill), binding discs (Rollabind), rub-ons (Making Memories), jute, netting, ribbon, staples, chip board, walnut ink (7 Gypsies), paint (Delta, Making Memories), diamond glaze (JudiKins), ink (Tsukineko), adhesive (3M), tag templates (Deluxe Designs), rubber stamps (River City Rubber Works), hole punch, square punch (Family Treasures), scissors, paper trimmer.

Page 93, What Makes us Friends Memory book by Rebecca Odom

Cardstock (Bazzill), patterned paper (7 Gypsies, KI Memories), photo turn (7 Gypsies), alphabets (Scrapworks), conchos (Scrapworks), ring fasteners, metal frames (Making Memories), eyelet letters (Making Memories), rub-ons (Making Memories), brads (Gary M. Burlin and Co.), foam tape squares (3M), adhesive (EK Success), ribbon (Offray), woven stickers (Me & My Big Ideas), ink (Tsukeniko), scissors, hole punch, paper trimmer.

Page 94, Wedding Memory Book by Jennifer Francis Bitto

Fabric, mat board, photos, ribbon, printed twill tape (7 Gypsies), brads, acorns, cardstock (Prism), patterned paper (Hero Arts, Autumn Leaves), game pieces, table of contents from an old wedding book, postage stamp (UK Design), reduced invitation, eyelets, envelope, dictionary text, oak leaf, tag (Avery), embossed acorns (Martha Stewart), heart clip (7 Gypsies), buttons, label (Me & My Big Ideas), fork charm, printed ribbon (Midori), personalized postage stamp (Martha Stewart), adhesive, ink, stamps (Postmodern Design, Wordsworth), scissors, paper trimmer.

Page 95, Enchantment Scrapbook Page by Stephanie McAtee

Tags (Making Memories), labels (Making Memories), acetate, cardstock (Prism), frames (7 Gypsies), book paper, ribbon, cardboard, ephemera, diamond glaze (JudiKins), paint (Making Memories), walnut ink, adhesive (3M), ink (Tsukineko), stamps (PSX), scissors, paper trimmer.

Page 96, Alice Triptych by Suzi Finer

Foam core, dried flowers (Pressed Petals), ribbon (May Arts), T pins (Prym-Dritz), decorative paper (Magenta, Design Originals), mesh (Magenta), dowel, coasters (River City Rubber Works), fluid acrylics (Golden), soft gel medium (Golden), foam tape squares (3M), diamond glaze (JudiKins), glue stick (3M), craft knife, paint brushes, sand paper.

Page 98, Wedding Memory Book by Marta Simmons-Weichmann

80# cover stock, medium and light weight vellum, 80 # text or 24# writing paper, PVC glue, vellum tape (3M), removable double sided tape (3M), craft knife, scoring tool, ruler, scissors, (for seven-hole pamphlet stitching.

Bookbinders awl, blunt tapestry needle, and linen thread or similar).

Page 99, Mexico Scrapbook Page by Rhonda Solomon

Cardstock (Prism), decorative papers (Pixie Press), stickers (Pixie Press, EK Success), button (Junk Itz), twine, ribbon, negative sheet protector, screen, acrylic paint, paint swatches, embossing powders, adhesive (3M), ink (Paintbox, Tsukineko), stamps (Making Memories, Hot Potato, Hero Arts, Stampendous), sewing machine, scissors, paper trimmer.

Page 103, Slash Pocket

Cardstock (Prism), adhesives (3M), scissors, paper trimmer, bone folder

Page 104, Discover Time Scrapbook Layout Template (see page 143), cardstock (Prism), raffia, overall buckles (Prym-Dritz), brads (Making Memories), safety pin (Making Memories), ink (Stampin' Up!), stamps (Stampers Anonymous), scissors, paper trimmer, craft knife, black writing pen, black permanent marker.

Page 106, Plastic Sleeve Pocket

Plastic sleeves, adhesive (3M) or attachments (thread, wire, brads, eyelets, staples, pins, paper clips, etc.), and scissors.

Page 107, Treasured Memories

Plastic sleeve protectors, papier-mâché chest, cardstock (Prism), mat board (black core), printed paper (Crafts, Etc) stickers (K & Co), adhesive (3M), foam square adhesive (3M), textured paint chips, acrylic paint, fiber (EK Success), square acrylic page bubbles (Making Memories), cardboard stencils (Headline), charms, markers (Sanford), inks (Tsukineko), binder combs, stamps (Stampers Anonymous), sponge daubers, paint brush, sea sponge, binder machine (Ibico), craft knife, scissors, paper trimmer.

Page 109, I Can See Clearly Pocket

Plastic page protectors, metal ruler or metal cookie cutter, heat tool with pointed tip (Walnut Hollow), glass cutting mat.

Page 110, Wish You Were Here Travel Folio

Mat board, decorative paper (K & Co), eyelets, woven stickers (Making Memories), stickers (K & Co), jute, laser cut surf board (Ariden Creations), printed acetate (K & Co),

page protector, miscellaneous beads, scissors, paper trimmer, eyelet setting tools (Readyset), heat tool with pointed tip (Walnut Hollow), metal ruler, glass cutting mat.

Page 112, Dueling Accordion Pullout

Cardstock (Prism), ink (Stampin' Up!), scissors, paper trimmer, bone folder, craft knife.

Page 113, The Perfect Journey Memory Book

Cardstock (Prism), clear tags (K & Co), rivets (Chatterbox), stencils (Headline), frame (Scrapworks), conchos, waxed fibers (Scrapworks), alphabet charms (Making Memories), photo flips (Making Memories), paper tags (Making Memories), washer words (Making Memories), label holders (Making Memories), ink (Ranger), black gesso (Golden), fluid acrylics (Golden), foam tape squares (3M), industrial-strength tape, scissors, hole punch, needle tool, black writing pen, bone folder, paper trimmer, sanding blocks or sand paper.

Page 115, Laminated Tag Pullout

Ephemera, luggage tags or lamination material (3M), hole punch, and scissors.

Page 116, Daisy's Memory Scrapbook Page

Cardstock (Prism), vellum (Prism), patterned paper (Anna Griffin), reduced copies of certificates, brads (Making Memories), laminating tags (3M), ink (Tsukineko), ball chain, mat board, reflective letter (Cole), twill tape (Wrights), adhesive (3M), vellum adhesive (3M), clear embossing powder, craft knife, sponge, stamps (Making Memories, Just Rite), scissors, paper cutter, computer for journaling.

Page 118, Tag Pouch Pullout

Cardstock (Prism), decorative paper, fasteners (Making Memories) or adhesive (3M), bone folder, hole and circle punches, scissors and paper trimmer.

Page 119, Reasons Why I Love You and Wedding Ensemble

Cardstock (Prism), vellum (Prism), printable acetate (3M), handmade paper, text weight paper, silver metal tape, brads (Making Memories), fibers, ribbon, ink (Tsukineko), absorbent ground medium, acrylic paint, label holder (Quickutz), alphabet and hinge die cuts (Quickutz), circle, seal, daisy punches, heart stamp (Stampin' Up!), daisy stamp, paint brush, sponge dauber, sanding block, bone folder, scissors, paper trimmer.

Page 122, Lock and Key Hiding Place
Cardstock (Prism), foam core, locks (National) or lock stickers (EK Success), ribbons, fiber, metal strips (Making Memories), hinges and hardware (National), craft knife or heat tool with blade attachment (Walnut Hollow), glass cutting mat, scissors, paper trimmer.

Page 123, Two By Two Memory Book
Cardstock (Prism), decorative paper (K & Co), mat board, rolled cork, stickers (K & Co), ribbon, decorative brads (Making Memories), metal embellishments, paper flowers (Making Memories), tassel, lock and key (National), metal hardware (National), small box, ink (Ranger), adhesive (3M), foam tape squares (3M), alphabet and fleur-de-lis die cuts (Quickutz), bone folder, sponge dauber, sanding block or sand paper, scissors, paper trimmer.

Page 125, Window Box Hiding Place
Cardstock (Prism), foam core, acetate or vellum, adhesive (3M), craft knife or heat tool with blade attachment (Walnut Hollow), glass cutting mat, scissors, paper trimmer.

Page 126, Estes Park Memories Altered Book
Old book, vellum (Prism), stickers (Anna Griffin, EK Success, Making Memories), feathers, brads (Making Memories), tags, printed ribbon (Making Memories), acetate,
fiber, ribbon, ink (Ranger), soft gel gloss (Golden), craft knife, metal ruler, needle tool, scissors.

Page 128, Rolled-Up Hiding Place
Fiber, wire, embellishment strips or paper scraps (Making Memories), adhesive (3M), needle tool, craft knife, and paper trimmer.

Page 129, Seashell from the Seashore Shadow Box Collage
Cardstock (Prism), vellum (K & Co), decorative paper (K & Co), black foam core, map, wire, raffia, tags, sea shells (US Shell), plastic letters, round tags (Avery), inks (Ranger), acrylic ground (Golden), absorbent ground medium (Golden), fluid acrylics (Golden), soft gel gloss (Golden), stamps, scissors, paper trimmer, paint brushes, shadow box frame, craft knife or heat tool with knife tip (Walnut Hollow), metal ruler, cutting mat.

Page 130, Clear Pocket Collage by Christine Adolph
Joss paper (Stampington & Co), tissue paper, linen (Ikea), organza (Ikea), silk, mesh, inkjet transparencies (Staples), stickers (K & Co), canvas board, gold interference paint (Golden), acrylic paint (Golden), soft gel (Golden), gold spray paint, adhesive (3M), stamp (Stampington & Co), sewing machine, scissors.

Page 131, Candy Bar Picks Scrapbook Page by Darcee Thompson
Vellum, baseball card holder sheet protector, cardstock (Prism), rub-ons (Creative Imaginations), snap, photo corner, paper clip (Making Memories), safety pin (Making Memories), stickers (Li'l Davis Design), fiber, texture frames, clear embossing ink, adhesive (3M), embossing powder, pearlescent powders (Jaquard), pen, chalk (Craf-T), heat tool (Walnut Hollow), embossing gun, scissors, paper trimmer.

Page 132, Ephemera Portfolio by Linda Blinn
Cardstock (Prism), papier-mâché portfolio (Stampington & Co.), printed black rubber bands (7 Gypsies), black embossed paper (K & Co), collected ephemera, art foil, elastics with metal tips (7 Gypsies), acetate transparencies (Apollo Transparency Film), black duct tape (3M), double-sided tape (3M), scissors, paper trimmer.

Page 133, Memories of Lost and Found Book by Tim Holtz
Cigar box, cardstock (Prism), fibers (Flights of Fancy Boutique), mica, embellishments (7 Gypsies, Li'l Davis, Making Memories), collected ephemera, ink (Ranger), glue (Crafter's Pick), metal foil tape, bone folder, stamps (Ma Vinci Reliquary), scissors, paper trimmer.

Page 134, Memory Scrapbook Page by Sharon Soneff
Cardstock (Stratford, Prism), patterned paper (Creative Imaginations), eyelets (Impress Rubber Stamps), brads (Lasting Impressions), label holders (Making Memories), tulle, metal embellishments, upholstery trims (Creative Imaginations), staples, thread, adhesive (3M), sewing machine, scissors, paper trimmer.

Page 135, Definitions Collage by Carol Wingert
Decorative paper (Autumn Leaves, 7 Gypsies, K & Co), nail heads (7 Gypsies, Magic Scraps), mini brads (Making Memories), stickers (Li'l Davis Designs), aluminum tag (Anima Designs), stretched canvas (Frederix), charm, hat pin, paper napkin, adhesive (3M), luggage tags (3M), ink (Clearsnap), paint (Plaid), foam stamps (Making Memories), scissors, paper trimmer.

Page 136, Envelope Journal by Lynne Perrella
Shipping envelopes, cardboard stencils, ephemera, twine and string, collage elements, wax, acrylic paints, mat medium, spiral-coil machine.

Page 136, Bee Journal by Michelle Ward
Brass charm (Fancifuls, Inc), honeycomb image (artist's drawing), mini brads, acetate, spiral journal, paints, copper tape, brushes, craft knife, alphabet stamp (A Stamp in the Hand).

Page 137, Precious Little Girls by Shannon Jones
Mini book (Making Memories), paper flowers (Making Memories), brads (Making Memories), patterned paper (Making Memories), ribbon, floss (DMC), buttons, lock and key, burlap, cardstock (Prism), eyelets, paint (Delta), adhesive (3M), chalks (Craf-T), foam stamps (Making Memories), stamps (Postmodern Design, Rubber Stampede), punches (Marvy Uchida, Family Treasures), scissors, paper trimmer.

resources

Most of the products used to make the art in this book are available from your locally owned scrapbook, stamp, and paper art stores. If they don't already carry the product you are looking for, in most cases, they should be able to order it for you. Please help keep these small independently owned stores open by giving them your business. They are the true heart of the industry.

Another good resource is your local arts and crafts superstore. While they don't specialize in paper arts, they do offer a wide selection of materials and can supplement your purchases from locally owned stores.

North America

Ben Franklin Crafts & Frames
262.681.7000
www.benfranklinstores.com

Hobby Lobby
405.745.1100
www.hobbylobby.com

Michaels
800.MICHAELS
www.michaels.com

UK

Hobbycraft
+44 0800 027 2387
www.hobbycraft.co.uk

Creative Crafts
+44 01962 856266
www.creativecrafts.co.uk

Australia

Eckersley's Arts, Crafts and Imaginations
+61 300 657 766
www.eckersleys.com.au

Website and/or contact information is provided below for the manufacturers of the products used in this book. Many of these websites either allow you to order directly (and ship internationally) or list stores where their products are available.

3M
www.3M.com
Adhesives including glue sticks, specialty tapes, foam tape squares, and spray adhesives; also transparencies and laminating supplies

7 Gypsies
www.7gypsies.com
Scrapbooking supplies including unusual embellishments

Above the Mark
www.abovethemark.com
Quality unmounted rubber stamp dies

Anima Designs
www.animadesigns.com
Unique artstamps, findings, ephemera, journals, found object jewelry, consignment gallery, journaling supplies, and more

Anna Griffin, Inc.
www.annagriffin.com
Fine decorative paper and embellishments for scrapbooking and paper arts

Apollo Transparency Film
www.apolloavproducts.com
Transparencies

Ariden Creations
www.aridencreations.com
Wood embellishments for scrapbook pages

Art Impressions
www.artimpressions.com
Original rubber stamps

Autumn Leaves
www.autumnleaves.com
Scrapbooking paper, books, and embellishments

Avery
www.avery.com
Office tags and supplies

Bazzill
www.bazzillbasics.com
Cardstock

Canson
www.canson.com
Archival photo organization including photo corners, albums, and papers

Carolee's Creations
www.carolees.com
Scrapbooking paper and embellishments

Chatterbox
www.chatterboxinc.com
Scrapbooking paper and embellishments

Clearsnap
www.clearsnap.com
Ink and rubber stamps manufacturer, including stamp wheels

Cloud 9
www.cloud9design.biz
Makers of Halo eyelet snaps

Colorbok
www.colorbok.com
Scrapbooking albums, paper, and embellishments

Craf-T
www.craf-tproducts.com
Rainbow chalk collection for paper arts embellishment

Crafters Pick
www.crafterspick.com
Makers of Ultimate glue

Crafts, etc.
www.craftsetc.com
Decorative and unique papers

Creative Imagination
www.cigift.com
Scrapbook papers, supplies, and embellishments

Delta
www.deltacrafts.com
Acrylic paints and craft supplies

Deluxe Designs
www.deluxecuts.com
Scrapbook papers, supplies, and embellishments

Design Originals
www.d-originals.com
Scrapbook papers, supplies, and embellishments; books

DiBona Designs
www.dibonadesigns.com
Fine artstamps

DMC
www.dmc.com
Embroidery thread and other fibers

DMD
www.dmdind.com
Paper and craft supplies

Dreamweaver Stencils
www.dreamweaverstencils.com
Brass templates and embossing supplies

Dymo
www.dymo.com
Label makers and supplies

EK Success
www.eksuccess.com
Scrapbook papers, supplies, and embellishments

Family Treasures
www.familytreasures.com
Paper punches

Fancifuls, Inc.
www.fancifulsinc.com
Brass charms and embellishments

Fiskars
www.fiskars.com
Scissors and cutting implements

Foofala
www.foofala.com
Scrapbook and paper art embellishments

Fred Mullet
www.fredbmullett.com
Quality nature artstamps

Frederix
www.fredrixartistcanvas.com
Artist canvas

Gary M. Burlin and Co.
www.garymburlin.com
Wholesale only—art and craft supplies

Glue Dots International
www.gluedotsinternational.com
Adhesive dots for paper craft applications

Golden
www.goldenpaints.com
Quality line of paints, fluid acrylics, and mediums for art

Headline
www.headlinesigns.com
Cardboard letter stencils

Hero Arts
www.heroarts.com
Artstamps

Hot Potatoes
www.hotpotatoes.com
Artstamps

Ibico
www.ibico.com
Binding machines and supplies

Ikea
www.ikea.com
Fabrics and housewares

Impress Rubber Stamps
www.impressrubberstamps.com

Jacquard
www.jacquardproducts.com
Artist paints and pearlescent powders

Jewelcraft
www.jewelcraft.biz
Embellishments including unique nailhead designs

Judikins
www.judikins.com
Stamps and supplies including Diamond Glaze

Just for Fun
www.jffstamps.com
Fine artstamps and supplies

Just Rite
www.justritestamps.com
Rubber date and letter stamps

K & Co.
www.kandcompany.com
Scrapbook paper, albums, and embellishments

KI Memories
www.kimemories.com
Scrapbook paper, supplies, and embellishments

Lasting Impressions
www.lastingimpressions.com
Brass templates and embossing supplies

Li'l Davis
www.lildavisdesigns.com
Scrapbook paper, supplies, and embellishments

Liquitex
www.liquitex.com
Paint and craft finishes

Ma Vinci's Reliquary
www.crafts.dm.net/mall/reliquary
Unmounted artstamps

Magic Scraps
www.magicscraps.com
Scrapbook embellishments and supplies

Making Memories
www.makingmemories.com
Scrapbook paper, tools, supplies, and embellishments

Martha Stewart
www.marthastewart.com
Home and craft supplies

Marvy Uchida
www.uchida.com
Markers and ink for paper crafting

May Arts
www.mayarts.com
Wholesale only—ribbons

Me and My Big Ideas
www.meandmybigideas.com
Scrapbook paper, supplies, and embellishments

Midori
www.midoriribbon.com
Ribbon, including printed varieties

National
www.natman.com
Hinges and hardware for unusual paper craft embellishments

Paper Parachute
www.paperparachute.com
Paper for paper art and scrapbooking

Paper Source
www.paper-source.com
Paper for paper art and scrapbooking

Papers by Catherine
www.papersbycatherine.com
Paper for paper art and scrapbooking

Pixie Press
www.pixiepress.com
Scrapbook papers and supplies

Plaid
www.plaidenterprises.com
Craft supplies including stamps, papers, and tools

PostModern Design
405.321.3176
postmoderndesign@aol.com
Artstamps

Pressed Petals
www.pressedpetals.com
Pressed flowers for embellishments

Prism
www.prismpapers.com
Large selection of fine cardstock for paper crafting, including exclusive textured line

Provocraft
www.provocraft.com
Coluzzle plastic template system

Prym-Dritz
www.prymdritz.com
Sewing notions and supplies

PSX
www.psxdesign.com
Artstamps and supplies

Purple Onion Designs
www.purpleoniondesigns.com
Artstamps and supplies

Quickutz
www.quickutz.com
Die-cut machine, unique alphabet and shaped dies

Ranger
www.rangerink.com
Rubber stamp and paper art inks and supplies

ReadySet
www.readysettools.com
Unique eyelet setting tool that can be used anywhere

River City Rubber Works
www.rivercityrubberworks.com
Artstamps with a humorous side and other unusual supplies

Rollabind
www.rollabind.com
Binding machines and supplies

Rubber Stampede
www.rubberstampede.com
Artstamps

Sakura
www.sakura.com
Markers and pens

Sanford
www.sanford.com
Maker of Sharpie markers

Scrapworks
www.scrapworks.com
Scrapbook paper, tools, supplies, and embellishments

Sizzix
www.sizzix.com
Personal die-cutting machine

Stampendous
www.stampendous.com
Artstamps

Stampin' Up!
www.stampinup.com
Home party artstamps

Stampington and Co.
www.stampington.com
Fine art and paper art supplies and books

Thermo Web
www.thermoweb.com
Adhesive

Tsukineko
www.tsukineko.com
Ink for rubber stamping and paper art

Tumblebeasts
www.tumblebeasts.com
Scrapbook stickers including unique textured stickers

Uhu
www.uhu.de
Glue sticks and adhesives

United Gilsonite Laboratories

www.ugl.com
Paint and finish sealers

US Shell

www.usshell.com
Shells and sea horses for craft and paper projects

Victorian Trading Co.

www.victoriantradingco.com
Victorian goods for the home and crafter

The Vintage Workshop

www.thevintageworkshop.com
Vintage clip art and printable surfaces for fabric and paper arts

Walnut Hollow

www.walnuthollow.com
Wood embellishments and wood & paper burning tools for scrapbook and paper arts

Westrim

www.westrimcrafts.com
Scrapbook and paper art embellishments

Wordsworth

www.wordsworthstamps.com
Paper, stamps and stencils for paper arts and scrapbooking

Wrights

www.wrights.com
Sewing trims

X-Acto

www.hunt-corp.com
X-Acto knives and blades

about the author

Although she's led a nomadic existence moving around the country with her wonderful husband and two beautiful young daughters, Jennifer Mason always makes her house a home by first unpacking her studio. Behind her studio door lie untold treasures and the promise of new friends made. She finds the quickest way to friendship is by sharing what she knows and loves.

Jennifer uses her degree in fine arts from the University of Michigan and her love of teaching to help others find their inner artist. She is regularly published in paper art and memory art magazines and books, including *Memory Makers, Legacy, Paper Crafts,* Anna Griffin's *Elegant Scrapbooking,* and *Sandi Genovese's Three-Dimensional Scrapbooks.* Her work has been featured in national print ads and on TV, including PBS, QVC, and HSN. Her style is always evolving but it is never without a touch of whimsy. Her love of color and typography is evident in her work.

Paper art is her first love, but she also enjoys painting murals, sewing, watercolor, knitting, jewelry design, calligraphy, crochet, and flower arranging. When she's not in her Keller, Texas, studio, Jennifer enjoys going to the park, the zoo, and on other adventures with her family.

acknowledgments

I would like to thank everyone who has ever helped or urged me along the artistic road but, as on the television broadcast awards shows, the music would start playing and names would be drowned out. So instead, I will thank those who have made the biggest difference in the culmination of this book and will send out happy thoughts to the rest.

To all of the fabulous artists who contributed to this book, my thanks go out to you for the excitement and creativity you each brought to this project. It was a gift to get to know you all a little better and to work on this book with you. Thanks for laughing *with* me when I sent out the email to tell you that I had dragged all your projects into the closet with me and my family when the tornado sirens told us to take cover.

To the wonderful people at Rockport who helped me through all the deadlines and setbacks, including when I tried breaking both of my ankles by stepping off a curb without looking while holding Stephanie McAtee's newly arrived project in my hand. Mary Ann Hall and Rochelle Bourgault have made writing this book fun!

To the police and EMTs who helped me find my daughter when I lost her (she was asleep on the couch covered with a blanket) and who came to the rescue when I had an unexpected seizure the week before the manuscript was due—thanks for keeping me safe and sane!

I must thank my parents (who never fully understand me but encourage me anyway, as long as I am happy) for providing me with the stacks of paper and crayons that started me creating young.

My thanks also to Missy and Jeff who have always been supportive of me and love me like a daughter (not like the crazy artist daughter-in-law that I really am).

I would like to thank my little girls, Becca Boo and Abba Roo, you guys make me want to be a better mommy. Thanks for letting me color with you!

I also thank Deb Sudbeck and Colorado Calendar Girls who always make me want to teach them something new. I will love you all forever for everything you are.

And finally to the two people who made this book possible from start to finish:

Jen VanSant, the very best friend a girl could have, thank you for helping me to conceive of the idea of this book and for giving it to me like it is. Namaste! Matt, the love of my life, for encouraging me, for taking such good care of our girls, for rubbing my swollen ankles, for calling 911 when I need it, for laughing at me, with me, and for me.